Angela Butler is just a
Having battled depression
more than once, she literall
and realised that the only p
things, was herself.

'I realised that I had spent years referring to myself as a 'Victim'. A Victim of other people's choices. A Victim of other people's actions. I asked myself the questions that we have all pondered at one time or another. Questions like 'why me?'. One day, it hit me – life will always be complicated. That's just the rhythm of life, it consists of ups and downs, positives and negatives – life is Bipolar! By reacting so sensitively to the ups and downs of life, I almost began to wonder whether I myself was Bipolar. But then it struck me – 'you cannot alter the direction of the wind, but you can always adjust your sails'. In other words, life will always throw cr*p our way, but it is only when you give up the reigns, stop trying to control life around you, and focus on your internal response to things, that real change can occur. We always have a choice. A choice of whether to act, or react. A choice to focus in the present moment and create the life that we desire. I took the power back and chose not to play the Victim for a moment longer. And there began this increadible and magical journey that transformed my way of thinking!'

Within 21 days, Angela had reprogrammed her subconscious, and friends and family began to ask her 'what's changed?'. Unable to sum things up in a sentence, she set about writing her 21 day programme, with the intention of sharing it only with close friends and family. The short writing exercise soon evolved into a full length book, which ironically, was complete in 21 days exactly.

Angela now lives her life, absorbed in the power and beauty of the present moment. As an inspirational, motivational writer, author and speaker, Angela intends to wake up and shake up, the attitudes of women the globe over.

With special thanks to

I would like to thank my Mum and Dad for their ongoing love and support. You have always believed in me, even when I did not believe in myself.

I would like to give a big hug and angel love, to my very special friend and mentor, Ali Campbell – for your support and advice during the creation of this book. You have believed in my heart and soul from day one. That is rare and you are special. I would also like to dedicate this book to Jean Campbell.

Big respect goes to Jimmy Lee Shreeve for encouraging me to take myself more seriously as a writer.

Much appreciation goes out to Joel Foster for creating the funky book cover!

Love goes to all of my family – my sisters, my brothers.

Special love to Nan who certainly influenced the production of this book and has always believed that 'one day she'll write a book but I don't know when'.

Love to Joseph and James

I don't even know where to start with my friends, as there are far too many of you to list each and every one of you, and I love you all in so many ways. But a big thankyou to Silvia, Emma, Philip, Kristina, Victoria ,Tracy and Sam for your encouragement.

I'd like to thank someone who I shall not name, for pushing me to actually get this done. Trying to stop me simply fuelled my determination.

This book is dedicated to all of my family members who are now angels, and is dedicated in particular to Caitlin Rose. I love you always.

Thankyou to those who I have met on my travels – the souls who have touched me, inspired me and totally 'got me'. To the strangers who are not yet friends, to the lovers who are forever embedded in my heart.

And to those who I cannot name – I love you, now and forever.

But the biggest thanks, should go to my Inner Goddess – for never giving up, for always believing – and for leading me to exactly where I am today. Publishing this book! Never give up on *your* dreams. Life is what YOU make it.

Unleash Your Inner GODDESS!

FROM VICTIM TO VIXEN
IN 21 DAYS AND BEYOND

Angela Butler

Crabtree Press

First Published by Crabtree Press in Great Britain in 2010
www.crabtreepress.com

Cover design by Joel Foster www.joelfoster.co.uk

Printed in Great Britain
by the MPG Books Group,
Bodmin and King's Lynn

A catalogue record for this book is available from, the British Library

For the latest information go to www.everywomanssecretweapon.co.uk

Sonia,

This book is dedicated to YOU. The most amazing woman on the planet. Who chooses not to play the Victim and finds a way to handle whatever life throws her way –

You cannot alter the direction of the wind, but you can always adjust your sails'

I would also like to dedicate to my Mum and Dad, for always believing that I would be where I am today.

To the Goddess within you ☺ Hope this adds some sparkle to your world,

much care

Angela xxx

CONTENTS

INTRODUCTION

Welcome to the little book that I hope will make big changes to your life, real change in as little as 21 days!

Who is this book for? Well, this book is specifically for YOU. If you are reading this, then trust me, you were led here by destiny and there is a message waiting for you to uncover. I know things have not always been sweetness and light for you.If they had you wouldn't be here but I strongly believe that we can and should learn something from everything in life. Even experiencing what we do not want and do not like, can lead us to reconfirming exactly what it is that we are looking for.

I do not sugar coat my advice, but the crack of my whip is always echoed with compassion. Life is too short for you to hide in the shadows. Think of me as the friend who only wants what is best for you, and 'tells it like it is'. Let's face it, we are all fed up with the friends who only ever say what they think we want to hear – right? You are here, because you have decided that it's time for something different, and so my aim, is to provide you with something 'real'. There may be moments where you feel a little 'uncomfortable'– but think about it like cleaning out a wound. We don't really want to go there but we know that it is necessary in order for healing to begin to take place. Hopefully, rather than being challenging, this book will simply whip you out from under the darkness and reveal to you what has always been there. As you read on, I'll hold a mirror up to you and shine a light upon you while guiding you gently along the journey. For any change to take place in our life, we more often than not, have to step outside of our comfort zone. Don't worry I've got you... you're totally safe.

But before, we begin on your life changing journey, I want to introduce you to the basic concept of this book in the easiest terms possible. This is not highbrow theory, this is what I *know* works!.

Throughout the book. I refer to the following characters: **the Victim,** her friends **chitter chatter** and **Fear, the Vixen,** and her best friend the **Inner Goddess**. What I want to make crystal clear from the word go, is that **all** of these characters live within YOU. They are ever present to a greater or lesser extent, and the majority of us throughout life, flit between playing the Vixen (you at your best) and the Victim (a role that you might have *chosen* to play!) The most common reason for becoming stuck between unhappiness and happiness, is the ever present interference of our internal chitter chatter and Fear.

Once we look at how you can choose not to play the role of the Victim ever again, and actively practise being the natural Vixen you really are on a daily basis, you will feel a powerful and real internal shift take place. Not only will you find that you almost 'drop your baggage at the door', together we are able to look at almost any life situation and break it down, exploring how our various characters would handle things.

This book guides you through three specific sections, and it is important to your well being that you read them coherently.

Please don't skip bits. This book is designed to guide you on your journey, with me as your coach to help along the way. While I can offer you the knowledge, the real change happens when you put it into action.

But don't worry, this is not just another 'self help' book that will wind up on your shelf amongst all of the others.

In fact, this book encourages you that *'less is more'*. Gone is the belief that if you are not happy with where you are at right now, then you need to *change*. Newsflash: you were perfectly fine just as you once were, just as you in fact ARE on the inside. You have probably just become 'lost' underneath the layers of life, issues and baggage that have accumulated over the years.

Once you begin to peel away these layers, once you realise that **'you cannot alter the direction of the wind, but you can always adjust your sails',** there is no longer any reason to ever resort to hiding behind the role of the Victim! You have complete control over your life, and how you act (rather than react) to things. In simply just 'being' and listening more to your Inner Goddess (and not chitter chatter, fear and everyone else around you) you are able to stay on *your* correct life path, and finally start living the life that you are destined for, without ever being sidetracked and bogged down.

But it doesn't end there – not only will you realise that YOU have the keys with which to unlock and access your authentic self, you are then also in a much better alignment with the omnipotent Universal energy.

You may or may not have heard of the Law of Attraction (it became big after the release of the book called 'the Secret' by Rhonda Byrne), – don't worry if you haven't. But once you work with the Law of Attraction, you discover that when you adjust your thoughts and feelings to work for you for a change, and focus on what you **do** want in life (rather than what you don't want, like so many of us do!) you can 'create' the dream into reality and actually manifest things that you have previously only dreamed of.

People around the world wish every day that they could put the law of attraction into action, I'll show you how you can really do it and why a lack of confidence in your own ability to make it work, might actually be the ONLY thing that holds you back from striking gold.

As this book helps you to Unleash your Inner Goddess, and find your most authentic self, you will be functioning daily, at your optimum level. You'll be oozing outward self confidence AND enjoying genuine inner peace. This is the ideal state from which to then work in harmony with the law of attraction, so what you have in your hands is really the 'Buy one, get one free bargain!' of the self improvement aisle.

Section One: lays down the solid foundations and principle teachings of the Inner Goddess Coaching programme. This is the philosophical part, the part that's essential to grasp before you can move fluidly along into the powerful change you'll experience in sections two and three. It's your life and your choices but I do recommend reading this book from start to finish, and then going back to randomly delve into it as and when you like, I'm sure you'll find yourself turning to section 3 in particular for future advice.

In Section One, we will look at the difference between the three roles: Victim, Vixen and Inner Goddess and define exactly what I mean when I use the term 'Goddess.' I will introduce you to the concept of your Inner Goddess as being your soul, your Inner spiritual energy, and then look at how this is connected to the omnipotent and omnipresent Universal energy. I also look at how we can use Source energy (the sun and moon) to re-charge your personal energy reserves in order to nourish our Inner Goddess and give and receive love and energy in abundance.

Section Two: Will guide you through a 21 day programme that will actually put the foundations of Section One 'into action'. You will see the philosophy *in action,* as this book is designed to put you in the driver's seat and to take a pro-active approach to self improvement. Psychologists determine that it takes 21 days to make or break a habit, and so our mission on this programme is to let go of limiting self belief and how you see yourself, 'break the habit' of thinking like a Victim and 'get into a good habit' of thinking and acting as a Vixen in tune with her Inner Goddess. Of course, you can continue to use the techniques and exercises that you will use over the course of the 21 days, for the rest of your life! This book life changing, beginning now and for the next 21 days and be*yond.*

Section Three: Offers a selection of potential every day scenarios such as 'The Goddess in Love', 'The Goddess at work', 'The Goddess and a break-up', and demonstrates the break down of how to handle such moments with the mindset of Vixen/Inner Goddess. Our goal is not to panic and resort back into the familiar role of the Victim. It also offers you solid techniques that can be used anytime, anyplace, when you need to instantly re-connect with your Inner Goddess.

At the back of the book is the 'Not so hidden', hidden chapter on The Inner Goddess and Sexuality. I wanted to keep this separate because I did not want the term 'Goddess' to become confused with the sexual connotations / ways that it can also be used by some other teachers. I also did not want this book to become too wrapped up with sex, because finding and unleashing your Inner Goddess, is about YOU feeling fabulous, regardless of whether or not you are in any kind of relationship!

The book is designed to guide you through a process, that is similar to my style of coaching, so don't expect everything to become clear right away – why would it?. This is a journey, and you may only piece it all together step by step. This book is pro-active – you need to engage with it, and complete the exercises, and use the tools, tasks and techniques that you shall create and discover along the way. Just reading it alone will not bring about or attract the changes that you desire. The real transformation comes from within YOU and this does not just stop once you reach the end of the book.

I truly hope, that this book will change your life forever and that you can return to its advice anytime you need me to remind you that your Inner Goddess is always with you – on the inside!

Before you begin your journey, just relax, safe in the knowledge that inside you truly are wonderful, just as you are. This is not about changing who you are, but slowing down, peeling off the layers of baggage, illusions and self created stories, and allowing your most authentic self to shine through. And when you shine, you give the sun a run for it's money lady!

We've all been in situations where someone else has made us light up... But remember when you shine a light on a diamond it's the diamond that does the sparkling. Now it's your turn as I turn the light of awareness towards you and show you what's been there all along.... Multi facetted and brilliant! Ready..?

Kick back, put your feet up, and let's begin the most exciting journey that you will ever take (oh okay, in a literary sense!)

I am blessed with your company and am with you every step of the way

Angela

'Show me the way to the Ocean!

Break these half measures.

these small containers!' – RUMI, from *Like this*

'Be your own lamp and be your own refuge' – Buddha

Set yourself free on the Ocean of Life!

Battle the darkness, don't block the light

Fear will guide you if you let it so

Follow your wisdom, to where you should go

Choosing the Victim will not let you see

The wonderful soul you were destined to be

Live as a Vixen, and see you are blessed

With your Inner Goddess, she'll handle the rest

Sailing along on the Ocean of Life,

You live in the moment, avoiding strife

With a heart that is open, a mind that is free

You love in abundance and learn how to 'be'.

Lighting the path on your journey of life

You don't fear the darkness, you embrace the light

And if negativity tries to take hold,

'In your darkest hour, you will find gold'.

If your Inner Goddess pretends she has failed

You laugh at the wind and you adjust your sails

It's time to start living, it's time to just to be

At one with your Goddess, so open and free!

It's time to try something different, that is why you are here. 'A life spent following the guidance of others, and doing what others expect of you, or what you think they expect of you, is a life spent fulfilling another's dreams – Buddha said be your own lamp and be your own refuge. Find inner peace within yourself and illuminate your own path – follow your dreams, it's time to stop merely *existing*, it's time to start LIVING' – Angela Butler

section one

Victim, Vixen or Goddess?

VICTIM, VIXEN OR GODDESS?

Which **role** will **you** choose for **your** life movie?

> **A loving crack of the whip #1:** *YOU are responsible for being exactly where you are right now. YOU have complete control over creating your destiny. If you are unhappy with where you are at then you need to change direction. 'If you keep doing what you have always done, you will keep getting what you have always got'. Grab life by the balls and stop playing the Victim!*

Victim, Vixen, Goddess – take a moment to consider what these words mean to YOU. This is not a test, do not worry about 'getting it right'. I like to think of it as being a little like 'holding a mirror up to you'. Through asking questions and getting you to reflect on your own beliefs, you are then able to compare and contrast this with the advice that I give you. Do not feel that you have to take all that I say at face value. I am simply a coach. I can re-frame things, and present them to you from a different viewpoint, but it is YOU who ultimately decides what is (or is not) right for you. You have the choice to live your life in whatever way you *choose* to, being whoever you *choose* to be. But always remember, that every moment, of every day, is a blank canvas, for you to decorate as you so wish.

Now, with there being no time like the present, I want you to dive right into the first exercise of the book.

Thinking back to what I just said about your life being like a movie, I want you to imagine that you have been given the opportunity to star as the leading lady in your very own 'life movie'! Snapping up the opportunity to pack your bags and head to Hollywood (hey, this is fantasy, so you may as well live a little) you receive an email from the writer, who is trying to gauge an impression of how you would like to be portrayed.

After attempting to sum yourself up, (whilst running up her International phone bill) she snaps *'look lady, would you class yourself as a Victim, or a Vixen, you know, the kind of Sassy kick ass woman, who is in tune with her Inner Goddess?'*

So… how exactly, do you answer this question? Do it, and do it now. No 'thinking it over' for any length of time, just run with your 'gut feeling', listen to your 'intuition' and write down on the line below, the word that came to mind, but take it one step further and complete the part of the statement that follows the word *because*.

I would describe myself as being a – ....Victim................

because ....I'm my own worst enemy........

Now, before reading too far ahead, look back at what you have just written, and say it out loud. Of course, if you are sat on the top deck of the number 57 bus, you might just want to shout it out in your head. But if the idea of 'coming out of the Victim/Vixen closet' makes you cringe with embarrassment, then you have to ask yourself *why?* It could be for a number of reasons – if you are a self confessed 'Victim' then this may just not sit right, and you feel that you have let yourself down somehow. If, on the other hand, you are a loud and proud Vixen (on impulse), after considering your reaction, perhaps you *then* questioned your choice? I know that as soon as I yelled out 'Vixen!' , I started to wonder whether I had a little too much confidence and began to wonder whether I would appear egotistical. I let my *chitter chatter* and *fear* of what other people   would think take over.

One thing that we need to clarify, right from the beginning, is that as you progress through this journey, you do not need to worry about what anyone other than YOURSELF thinks. Stop second guessing what goes on in your head, because that very action is what this book is trying to eradicate. When you choose to ignore, or silence that inner voice, you are actually stifling your INNER GODDESS. The only person who will know what you answer, is you, and it is vital that you are honest with yourself every step of the way in order to get the results that quite frankly, you are entitled to.

So – I now want you to think about how your chosen role has made you feel, and write your thoughts in the space below. Let your Inner Goddess speak.

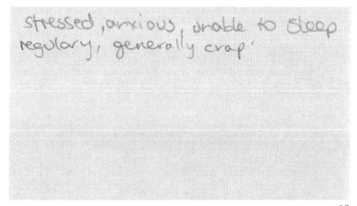

stressed, anxious, unable to sleep
regulary, generally crap.

I appreciate, that this is just the beginning and that I am yet to describe to you how I define the characters. I simply wanted to get you thinking about what YOUR initial feelings were, and now that you have done that, we are going to take a closer look at the three roles, The Victim, The Vixen (and her Inner Goddess) and look at how and why we all switch between all three as we venture through life. Note, that I will sometimes say The Vixen in tune with her Inner Goddess, but at other times I may refer to solely the Vixen, and the Inner Goddess, as two separate entities. This is because in an ideal world, a Vixen (you) would work in harmony with her Inner Goddess (soul, spirit, inner energy, intuition, whatever YOU want to call it) but in reality, it is easy for the two to become disconnected.

So, let's start by looking at the role of the Victim.

MEET 'THE VICTIM'

Loving crack of the whip #2: *The Victim is a role that you choose to play at any given time. As soon as you find yourself playing that role, make an active choice **not** to play it. You can only be a Victim if you have no choice – you always have a choice. A choice to how you choose to react or act on something. Even doing nothing is a choice. Whether it is passive or active, you have the power and choice to handle things from a different perspective. Every second is the chance to start over.*

Now I know that this statement may rub some of you up the wrong way but I do not sugar coat my advice, as that simply wastes time. I reached the above conclusion after adopting the motto that **'you cannot alter the direction of the wind, but you can always adjust your sails'**.

The sooner you grasp this concept, the better your life can be. Think about it…

It does *not* matter what life throws at you, because you can always *choose* how you deal with it. You are the one in control of the sails. Whether you choose to deal with it, or not deal it, that is still an active choice. Therefore, you cannot be a 'Victim' because this indicates that you are powerless, *but you are not.*

Now, I hear some of you thinking 'yes but I was abused, I lost my mother, or father, or child' (insert your personal worst experience here). I did not ask for these things to happen to me, and I cannot control whether such things happen again, The pain that I felt was the worst thing that I have ever experienced in my life, and how was I supposed to just handle that? If you are going to start telling me that I should have dealt with it effortlessly then I am going to throw this book in the nearest trash can and…'

And *breathe*. Let me explain further.

In the motto above, the wind, is life. You cannot control life, and life is a cycle of ups and downs, positive and negatives, good and bad, joy and pain, love and loss.

No matter how hard you try to control it, there is just no chance of succeeding. So why is it, that so many of us spend our lives battling life, battling FEAR? We become so wrapped up in the what ifs, that they consume the present, and shape our reality. I will come onto this a little later, how thoughts and feelings actually become reality. For now, I want you to just take a moment, and jot down (and be honest, this is just between you and yourself!) just what it is that scares you the most about life? What are your deepest and darkest fears?

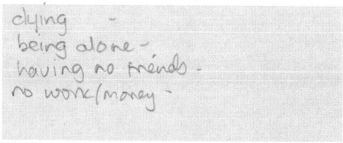

To help show the transition of eradicating fears further in this chapter, I am going to open up and share some of mine with you. Then we're in this together

I fear: losing my parents, having no money, finding love and losing it through simply being myself, and being struck down with an incurable illness.

Let's look at this little list (and yours) *logically*. Will all of the worrying in the world actually stop any of these things from possibly happening? No*!*

In fact, worrying may actually bring on the occurrence of several things on my list. For instance; worry, lack of sleep and stress can bring on depression, which could result in me losing my job, and this in turn would bring about having no money. The mind has an incredible power over our physical body, and our thoughts and feelings shape our reality. So worrying about being struck down by an incurable illness may actually run down my immune system (again, sleepless nights and stress), cause my body to go out of whack and develop cancer or something as equally as horrifying. Do you see ?

Let's take a little moment to look at the word disease. Those of you familiar with the work of Louise L Hay, will know that physical illness, disease comes from just that – **dis-ease**. Being uneasy! Holding onto worry, fear and any other negative emotion, simply makes you sick. In worst case scenarios, it can even shorten your life! So in trying to control your destiny, in gripping on so tightly that you cause yourself stress, you are actually adding fuel to a run away train on a down hill route to your worst nightmares.

We can do a lot to change our own reality, you have more power in that than you may be aware of, and I will soon come to explain to you, just how a little something called 'the law of attraction' really is the **secret** to life.

But: you may be able to do things to change the amount of the control that *you* have over *your* life, but you cannot control the lives of those around you. It really is up to them! And so, there will always be risks that something bad may happen to someone close to us, there will always be the very real possibility of losing our family, or the one that we love. I'm afraid to say that this is just a part of life. However, we can alter how we respond to such events in our lives, and choose to *act* rather than *react*.

A Victim reacts. A Vixen in tune with her Inner Goddess acts.

Before I go further, I want you to just pause for a moment, and focus on the statement above. A good tip, is to have a block of post it notes handy as you read this book, and jot down any pointers that you find inspirational and then stick them somewhere that you will see them daily.

'A Victim reacts. A Vixen in tune with her Inner Goddess acts'. What is the difference between *reacting* and *acting?*

Reaction is something that we do on impulse. Often, it is an action that it is fed by emotion, and more often than not, a lack of logical thought. Reactions are not always a bad thing. They can after all, potentially save our life in emergency situations. But when it comes to relationships with others, and matters of the heart for example, to simply react on every feeling or emotion that you have, there and then, can lead to subsequent regret and problems further down the line. How many times, have you woken the morning after the night before, and felt that surge of dread in the pit of your stomach, when you realise that you totally over reacted and wish that you had just gone home and slept on it?

A Vixen in-tune with her Inner Goddess, knows, that nothing, no matter how big, needs to be solved in the immediate moment. Not unless it *is* a matter of life and death. It may seem like you are 'slowing things down' by stepping back initially, and taking time to just 'be' (rather than think). But in the long run, this can actually be more effective, and save you time. Stepping back and just being means that you do not crowd your mind with 'he said, she said, what if this and what if that?' (again, FEAR – the ever present internal chitter chatter). You have inner peace and clarity and the answers will soon come, as you are able to hear your Inner Goddess.

We all need to learn to stop listening to FEAR, and the opinions of others, and just trust our Inner Goddess.

It really will be okay, and it is that simple. I want you to breathe, relax, and enjoy the concept, that you are safe to 'just be'. You are not alone. You have your Inner Goddess who is always present within you. Like your internal Sat Nav, she guides you. You will get from A to B, and you do not need to be distracted by the internal obstacles – your false friend FEAR, your internal chitter chatter, or the external obstacles – life events (the wind) that you cannot control, the opinions of others.

You now have the knowledge of the battle that the Inner Goddess faces in life, and how she is repressed and smothered by the competing and envious army of fear, and friends. You can differentiate between the different voices, and know which one to listen to!

So – we have covered the role of the Victim, let's look at the Vixen.

MEET 'THE VIXEN'

Loving crack of the whip #3: *The Vixen is you when you are being true to yourself. To not be true to yourself is an active choice. If you are stuck in the role of the Victim then it is up to YOU to take a proactive approach to 'waking up' and smelling the coffee. Life is too short to smother your soul.*

The Vixen, quite simply put, is **'you on a good day'**. You know the you that I am talking about.

You, when you are simply relaxed, and comfortable with who you are and where you are at in life. I am not suggesting that a Vixen is some out of reach, far fetched sex kitten. This is not about how you look on the outside, but who you are on the inside. How you project your internal self upon your external surroundings and the people in your life.

The Vixen, is you when you are not *choosing* to play the role of the Victim. She is the you, who accepts herself just as she is, the good *and* the bad. She is comfortable with her past, is happy to just 'be' in the present, and has the knowledge that she can shape and create her future, by using the power of her mind (thoughts and feelings) and listening to her Inner Goddess – allowing her internal Sat Nav to guide the way and sail the ship that is herself, on the ever unpredictable ocean of life.

Once you master how to tear off the chains that you have placed around yourself – and stop choosing to play the role of the Victim, the Vixen emerges, like a mermaid stepping out of the ocean, ready to embrace and challenge the world.

That is all there is to it.

I am not about to tell you that you must completely change who you are, in order to now become a Vixen. If you hoped that it would involve a lot of strenuous, hard, time consuming work, then you are in the wrong book! The Vixen is YOU and that is all there is to it, and you are fine just as you are, *flaws and all*. In becoming a Vixen, learning to Unleash her Inner Goddess, you are not looking to transform yourself into an unrealistic supermodel slash Stepford wife. No! You are metaphorically (and excuse my turn of phrase here but it says it best) 'sticking your fingers up to society, the media, anyone and everyone who has led you to believe that YOU are not good enough. That you should be more. That you should be thinner, more successful, have bigger breasts, whiter teeth,and be a whore in the bedroom and a Madonna in the family room.'

You are accepting yourself, just as you are, safe in the knowledge that you will never be perfect, and nor should you want to be! There is no such thing as the 'perfect woman' *or* the perfect man for that matter. Those who may appear to be perfect on the outside, often have a ton of misery going on on the inside. It's all an illusion, and you know that if you are honest with yourself.

This is about you allowing yourself to finally be you, in all your glory. To listen to your Inner Goddess, and not stifle her for a moment longer. Being you, really is okay. You are safe. Whatever life throws at you (and boy, it will!), you *can* and *will* survive. That is what we do.

And…breathe!

MEET THE 'INNER GODDESS'

Loving crack of the whip #4: *Your Inner Goddess is the only truth that you can base your life upon. A life built on anything less is a life built on rocky foundations. It's just a matter of time until the whole lot comes tumbling down.*

The simplest and most basic meaning of the symbol of the Goddess is the acknowledgement of the legitimacy of female power as a beneficent and independent power. – Carol P. Christ

'We all have within us, an Inner Goddess'

Your Inner Goddess, is your most authentic self. Your soul. Your intuition. Your heart. The real, true essence of YOU. Simple!

And the trick to unleashing her, is to simply learn how to quieten the hustle and bustle that confuses her, dig her out from underneath all of life's baggage that has accumulated and let her **JUST BE!**

That's it! You do not need to invent your Goddess. The Goddess, is not an unrealistic, society defined role model that you should be living up to. **Your Goddess is simply YOU**, regardless of your looks, weight, race, sexuality or age. The world would be a pretty boring place if we were all the same wouldn't it.

In fact, the beauty of 'Unleashing your Inner Goddess' is that **the less you do, the better.**

Think of your Inner Goddess as being like your very own internal Sat Nav. She can alert you as to when you are veering off your life path, or she can wait for your commandments, and take you to exactly where you want to go. But the most important thing that you need to know this far into the book, is that although we all have an Inner Goddess, who is already perfectly fine, just as she is – we often do not hear her, because the ever present hum drum made by chitter chatter and Fear. These two characters accompany or at least lead to the formation of the role of the Victim. It is our mission to stop them from taking hold, and give the Inner Goddess a real chance to finally be heard.

It is not just chitter chatter and Fear that drown out the Goddess' voice. How many times do you hear her speak, but question her, over analyse, or seek approval of others, before you trust her advice as given? Again, we do such things, because we fear that if we trust our inner voice, and things go wrong, then we will only have ourselves to blame. But as soon as we grasp the reality, that 'you cannot alter the direction of the wind but you can always adjust your sails', then it becomes clear that there really is very little to fear in life. No matter what happens, we will deal with it and find an alternative route on the journey of life. And in listening to fear, we are wading in murky waters anyway, because this means that we are operating at a fraction of our true potential. At least by listening to our Inner Goddess, we know, that if we do veer off track, we must still be on the right path, we have just taken a detour, because life has in store for us, something we cannot yet see.

Until you embrace and accept your Inner Goddess in all her glory, you simply will never know just what you are capable of, or fulfil your true destiny. In Section two, I begin the process of Unleashing your Inner Goddess by helping you to identify, meet and engage with your Inner Goddess in as short a time as possible. Once you have done so, it will be almost impossible to revert back to playing the Victim.

Your Inner Goddess, can also be thought of in terms of an **energy**. Throughout this book, I will look at how you can re-charge this energy, using Universal energy, and also how your Inner Goddess, can also give energy to others. In order for her to work to her optimum efficiency, she needs to be nurtured and treated with respect. When we run ourselves ragged, we are drained of our energy, and this is when we are most vulnerable to becoming run down, and susceptible to veering off course and heading towards Victim City! Taking care of your Inner Goddess on a daily basis is something that we look at in the 21 day programme in section two of this book, and also in the maintenance programme in section three. It's not just a case of 'Unleashing your Inner Goddess' and that's that..I want you to make subtle changes to the way that you live your life, so that you will transform your bigger picture.

Of course, the first thing that we will look at, is how to drop the backpack of baggage that you have been carrying around with you, Until such things are removed, your Goddess stands no chance. We will peel away your layers, zap away the Victim, and give the Vixen a good scrub.Only then can you Unleash your Inner Goddess and then it is your solo mission to keep communicating with her daily. Life will never be the same again. Once you master how to monitor your inner and emotional energy and health, you will keep on top of things as you go along and won't ever find yourself succumbing to the lure of the Victim again. You will have all of the tools and knowledge from this book, to respond to anything that life throws at you. Never forget that 'You cannot alter the direction of the wind, but you can always adjust your sails'. One glance at this motto will snap you back into focus.

A second glance at the Goddess

Before continuing, I would like to think about the word Goddess for a moment, because there are several ways that the word can be used and I want you to consider these, so that you form a version that you are most comfortable with.

Religions and schools of thought often use the term 'Goddess' to refer to a deity. Something sacred and powerful. There can be Goddess' of all manner of things, Venus the Goddess of Love. Hindu Goddesses who guide you via dreams, you name it, there is likely a Goddess for it somewhere. But the most powerful Goddess that I believe in, is the Lunar Goddess – the Moon.

Then there are the more sexual implications of the term Goddess. In the dark and mysterious world of Fetish, the Mistress may often be referred to a Goddess, who is worshipped by her Submissive. The art of Tantra talks about the Goddess, and Goddess energy, as does the field of Kundalini energy.

But all of these possibilities aside, I believe, that we all have within us, an **Inner Goddess.** And I link this Goddess, to the Universal energy, in particular, the Sun and the Moon. All that Goddess figures serve to do, is give you the back up, that self belief, so that you feel protected in listening to your Inner wisdom, They take you on an internal, spiritual voyage. But rather than begin this voyage, by looking outside of yourself for the guidance, why not just trust your Inner Voice? Why seek the help of fictional goddesses when you have the most powerful one of all, existing deep within your own physical body?

Fear is of course the main reason why so many of us prefer to look to external sources for validation of our life choices and happiness. It gives us support, confidence and makes us feel less alone – it also means that we can throw caution to the wind and use the safety net / protective shield of 'oh well, it wasn't meant to be' if and when we do not wind up where we want to go. But when you remind yourself daily, that **'you cannot alter the direction of the wind, but you can always adjust your sails'** you begin to realise that you do not need to look to an external source for that security. You already have it, deep within yourself. And the path that is the life that you lead, will never be a straight path carved of stone. It is curvy and bumpy, and you may not always just get right from A to B. *But this is perfectly okay.*

What if life is supposed to be complex and colourful? What if it is through experiencing the mistakes, the bad times and the sad times, that we truly find out who we are and what we are made of? Without experiencing darkness, we cannot appreciate or define light. The world is made up of endless contrasts, like yin and yang, these polar opposites need to co-exist for there to be balance. So accepting that quite frankly, life WILL continue to throw crap at you, sort of takes away the power and fear of 'things going wrong'. It is not things going wrong that is the issue, but how you can or cannot handle them. But knowing that you simply need to adjust your sails, gives you an Inner calmness, that begins to soothe this fear.

Once you allow your own Goddess to breathe, she begins to come back to life. Her strength is nourished and she is an unstoppable force. But she is not alone, and neither are you. You see, as I will cover in Section Two (in an exercise called 'Meet your Inner Goddess') Your Inner Goddess is like your own best friend. The Vixen co-exists with her, they work in Unison. But not only that, your Goddess also works in harmony with the Universe. Some call this Universal energy 'Source energy' and others call it life force, or chi. In the study of the 'Law of Attraction' we are taught that when we combine our internal energy (Inner Goddess) with this Universal energy, we can slide into 'the flow' and everything that was destined for our life comes to us *effortlessly*.

You see, life really shouldn't be, and doesn't have to be, an endless, meaningless struggle. Give yourself permission to allow your Goddess to guide you and find yourself 'in the flow' of the Universal energy.

Through-out this book, I will provide you with further detail on the relationship between your Inner Goddess and the Universal energy, so do not worry too much about grasping this concept wholly this minute. But play around with the idea, and see how it sits with you. Before moving on, I want us to look at the Sun and Moon and the role that they can play, in nourishing your

Inner Goddess, as this will give you a clearer picture as to just how we can connect to the Universal energy, because what most of us who are familiar with such ideas struggle with, is the actual doing rather than the knowing. It is the same with the Law of Attraction – after the book 'The Secret' was read by billions worldwide, the number one question was 'so I know about the secret – but how do I put it into action?' People knew the fundamentals but needed clearer step by step examples and exercises to follow in order to move passive information into active energy.

Rather than have this book be another over complicated compilation of theory, I want you to just relax into it, and 'go with the flow'. I will actively guide you through tools, techniques and exercises in Section two, the 21 day programme, so that you find yourself unlocking your energy, your Inner Goddess, and your potential effortlessly. Try not to worry too much about *why* you are doing something, and allow yourself to just do it.

The Sun and Moon – your personal chargers

Solar and Lunar energy powers the Universe. Without the Sun, we would not know day, and without the moon we would not know night. Simple.

A **solar deity** (also **sun god(dess)**) is a deity who represents the sun, or an aspect of it, usually by its perceived power and strength (Wikipedia). Religions and schools of belief have all manner of Gods and Goddesses related to the sun, but I do not want to spend too long on listing them here and now, as in a way, it is irrelevant to what we will be covering. But one particular fact that caught my attention, was that in Egyptian times, there was a Neolithic concept of the sun as being this energy force, that travelled the sky in a boat, along with Ra and Horus. Compare this image, to one of your energy as being similar to the sun within a boat, except the boat is your physical body, and you sail on the Ocean of Life.

With the ups and downs of daily life, we find ourselves becoming low in personal energy from time to time. It happens to the best of us, to all of us. But for women in particular, with playing the numerous roles that we play on a day to day basis, and often being seen as the primary care giver, we can often find ourselves drained from giving. Now, I am not about to suggest that you stop giving, and become a little selfish. But when you experience a slump in your personal bank of energy, you are no good to anyone. Therefore, taking time out, to take care of YOU, before you care for others, is essential, so that you are not only happier in yourself, but you are also better equipped to give a richer energy to those around you. Think of it like a car running without any petrol. You would not ignore the petrol gauge, telling you that it's time to fill up on energy. Well you are no different.

I will look at this subject in Sections two and three, it runs throughout the book, so don't worry too much about how you can utilise the solar energy in this moment, but just trust me when I say that you can. I will guide you through meditations and visualisation techniques, that enable you to recharge your Inner Goddess/ energy at any time of the day, in any place, simply by tuning into the sun, and allowing it to penetrate your soul. For those of you familiar with energy practise, and healing, think of Reiki, or the art of Kundalini. There is a constant flow of giving and receiving between your energy and the Universal energy. You can absorb energy, and you can conserve energy, you can give out energy and you can share and build energy (this is particularly useful in relationships). Keep your personal levels topped up through connecting to the Universe, via the sun and the moon. This Universal flow is never ending and once you feel connected to it, you are then able to work with the Law of Attraction, and lose yourself in the flow that is life. Remember that living should be effortless.

The Moon works in a similar way to the Sun, but I like to think of the Moon as having extra special, potent energies that are specifically designed for nourishing the female of the species.

Our great symbol for the Goddess is the moon, whose three aspects reflect the three stages in women's lives and whose cycles of waxing and waning coincide with women's menstrual cycles. – Carol P. Christ

Through working out the current moon phase at the time of reading this book, you will be able to understand with greater clarity, just how the all powerful Luna Goddess could be affecting your energy levels and work with her accordingly. Again, I provide an exercise in Section Two, that teaches you how to connect to the power of the Moon in order to replenish your energy, but also as a way to conserve the energy supplies that you gathered during the day, from the energy of the Sun. All that I want you to take with you right here, right now, as we glide into the next topic, is to understand that you are a vital cog in the wonderful machine that is the Universe as we know it. Never ever doubt the role that you play, in keeping the Universal energy flowing. People are like receptors, who absorb the energy, whip it up, strengthen it, and then pass it on. Through keeping in tune with your Inner Goddess, and nourishing her daily, you are in turn, feeding the Universal energy with a positive stream, and this is also blissful for those around you. When you choose to focus on the past, the negative, and give rise to the Victim, then you disengage from this flow, you interrupt this state of bliss, and not only do you let yourself down, you can also affect those around you.

It really is simple – we get no rewards in life for choosing to play the Victim. The world is entering a 'spiritual awakening' and it is through energy that we can truly connect, and begin to make a difference. When times are hard, focus on the bigger picture and remember that you are a child of the Universe. If you disconnect yourself from the flow, you are going to feel off kilter. Fact. The choice is yours. On that note, I think that it is time for us to sail into the topic of the relationship between your Inner Goddess and the Universe, and look at how she can guide you to exactly where you want to go, when you learn how to work with the flow.

INNER GODDESS – YOUR INTERNAL SAT NAV! WHERE WILL YOURS TAKE YOU?

> **Loving crack of the whip #5:** *Your Inner Goddess can take you to where your heart desires. If you are not exactly where you want to be, then you have to ask YOURSELF why.*

Just where will your Inner Goddess take you?

Now that you are familiar with the idea of playing the role of Vixen, with daily communication with your Inner Goddess, I want you to think about how the Inner Goddess relates to the outside world.

We have established, that if you just relax, and listen to your Inner Goddess, then she will function like an inner Sat Nav, and will take you to exactly where you want to go.

But in order for her to do that, we need to look at how the Inner Goddess works. Firstly, there is the side of her that is often known as 'Intuition'. I like to think of this as the factory default settings to the Sat Nav. This is the part of the IG that is designed to work in an emergency and prevent the Vixen from getting completely lost in life.

Be honest – how often do you listen to your intuition? I don't mean listen, but really *listen*. Again, remember, that this journey is simply between you and yourself, so you can be as brutally honest as possible here. Do you follow what your intuition tells you to do, every single time? Or do you often silence it, and do what your head instructs you to do, being controlled and directed by the Victim's buddies, chitter chatter and fear?

If you listened to your intuition, or your Inner Goddess more often, how much of a difference do you think it would make to your life? Which brings me onto this little but ever so vital question, *'just what is it that makes us so resistant to actually listening to our Inner Goddess?'*

'We often resist listening to our Inner Goddess and intuition, through FEAR of things going wrong, and having nothing to blame it on but ourselves'.

And there we have it. Up pops our faithful friend Fear again! If we choose (and yes again, it is a choice) to ignore our intuition and listen to the advice of our friends chitter chatter, fear and those around us, if and when things go hideously wrong, we can always point the finger at something or someone else. We can almost console ourselves, with the knowledge, that we didn't quite give it our best shot. We were overcome by fear, it was not our fault. Whereas, if we were to take 100% personal responsibility for our choice, and the results or consequences that followed, where would we be if things didn't work out as planned?

'Where would we be, if things didn't work out as planned, when following our intuition / Inner Goddess?'

Seriously? Well, we would actually be in a much better position than if we had allowed fear to over-ride us, that's for sure! Okay, so if we were in the latter position, we could at least blame something right? But all that blame only serves to put yourself back into the very role that we are aiming to shed once and for all! The role of the Victim!

It's time to wake up and shake up, get that Inner Goddess activated and raring to go, and just trust her! So what if things don't go as planned? It does not mean that they have necessarily gone wrong. Just be safe in the knowledge, that your intuition's main aim, is to keep you on your personal life path and stop you from veering too far off course. Just because it may guide you down an avenue that you had not anticipated, this does not mean that you were not supposed to wind up there. It just means that life had something in store for you that you could not yet see.

But no matter where you wind up, always remember 'you cannot alter the direction of the wind, but you can always adjust your sails'. Sometimes, the unexpected diversions, are where you will meet the love of your life, your new best friend, or a contact for your dream job. Be open to the endless possibilities of the unknown.

I mentioned that the Inner Goddess (Sat Nav) can be split into two parts, and the second part is the side to the Goddess, that can be 'programmed'. Imagine how wonderful it could be, if you could physically take a keypad every night before bed, and type in your wildest dreams and desires. Ranging from how you'd like the next day to pan out, to how you'd like the next year to unfold! Well, there is of course, no literal 'key pad' for programming your Inner Goddess, but you can mentally feed your Goddess with all of the information required in order for it to take you where you want to go.

You may (or may not) have heard of 'the secret', to life, otherwise known as 'The Law of Attraction'? It simply states, that 'what you focus on grows'. For example, you want more money, but you spend all your time focusing on your want, need, that stems from a lack of money. The law of attraction continues to deliver you debt, because it works on the principle, that 'like attracts like'. It cannot differentiate between what you do want, and what you don't want. It simply responds according to your 'feelings'.

Now let's break it down. Thoughts, feed our subconscious mind. And from here, our Inner Goddess is programmed. Okay, re-read that sentence again and really let it sink in;

'thoughts feed our subconscious mind, and from here, our Inner Goddess is programmed'.

Whatever you have programmed into your Sat Nav (Inner Goddess), this will generate a route for the Vixen to follow. Powered by her Inner Goddess, she will be taken to exactly where the energy created inside (feelings) directs her. If she veers off course, crashes, or winds up in the completely wrong place to where she originally intended, then the only person to blame, is herself. And we don't do blame now do we, because that is behaviour of the Victim. So with this bolder mindset in tow, the Vixen is confident, in programming her Inner Goddess and trusting that it will take her to where she wants to go.

With this unmovable belief and trust in the Inner Goddess capability to work in synchronicity and harmony with the Universe, the Vixen can sit back and relax, and know that she is already on her way to living the life that she desires.

Of course – it is not as simple as sitting back and waiting for life to unfold. The Inner Goddess continues to guide the Vixen, every minute, of every hour, of every day. It presents her with information, ideas, inspiration, motivation – that is all communicated via the first part of the Goddess that we looked at ; 'intuition' .If the Vixen does not listen to such messages, then she will of course, find herself off the beaten track, and it is down to herself to get herself back on track.

But it really is all much more simple than you are probably currently thinking. You see, all this takes, is faith and trust. So why is that so difficult for so many of us to assert? Do we even have to answer this question? Let's see who yells it out first... FEAR!

So, now you have a greater insight into how the Inner Goddess functions on a practical level. Let's take a look at beginning to work in harmony with your Inner Goddess!

VIXEN AND INNER GODDESS V THE VICTIM

The never ending courtship between YOU, your Inner Goddess, with the odd interference from the Victim

Imagine that there are 3 characters in a rowing boat, floating along on the Ocean of life. The Victim, The Vixen and the Inner Goddess. Now, picture the scene – on a beautiful sunny day, the boat is hi-jacked by Fear and Chitter Chatter and things become complicated. The Vixen wants to paddle effortlessly, and go with the flow of the Ocean of life. But Fear and Chitter Chatter begin to put doubts in her mind, and she begins to worry. She worries that she may not survive the journey without capsizing. She fears stormy weather that may knock her off course. At the front of the boat, Inner Goddess attempts to explain to the Vixen that *in the Ocean of life, there is nothing to fear.* There is no such thing as drowning, in fact, diving right into the depths of the water is where the fun begins. As for stormy weather, the boat is well equipped to survive. They can simply adjust their sails and a detour is part of the adventure. Who knows where they may end up, and who they may meet along the way. But the Vixen is so distracted by the ever growing noise that her enemies are making, that she cannot even hear Inner Goddess. Finally, the Goddess gives up, and collapses from the strain of trying. Fear and Chitter Chatter take over, and the Vixen, drained from this experience, simply throws down her oar, and turns to the Victim and insists that she take over. Victim asks 'why me?', and before she knows what has hit her, Chitter Chatter and Fear have knocked her over, and are sitting on top of her, completely in charge of the navigation.

With such complete and utter chaos at the helm, the boat begins to wobble. With no one really focusing on direction, they find themselves being tossed around by the waves of the Ocean of life. Victim desperately struggles to fight her way out from her predicament, whilst Vixen remains crumpled in a ball in the corner, wondering if and when Vixen will regain control of things. A huge wave crashes on top of the boat, and Inner Goddess is left clinging on for dear life,and Fear and Chitter are swept on top of the Vixen. Victim gains composure and finally has control of the oars, but Vixen is not willing to simply give away her power. Battling with her enemies, she finally manages to throw Fear and Chitter Chatter overboard, and the Victim is pushed into the Ocean which gives rise to hope, for the Inner Goddess.

Vixen regains composure, and in the silence that pursues, can finally hear Inner Goddess, who lovingly guides her back onto calm water. What the two aren't aware of, is that Victim and her friends Chitter Chatter and Fear have somehow managed to cling onto the ledge on the side of the boat, but Inner Goddess soon figures this out, and vows to keep an eye on them. Vixen trusts the Goddess 100 % in doing so, and admits that she really needs to make more time and effort, to actually listen to what her one true friend has to say. For as long as Vixen sticks to this promise, the journey on the Ocean of life should be effortless.

Think about YOURSELF as being the boat., A vessel, that contains all three of these characters, with the ever present threat of being invaded by Chitter Chatter and Fear. You have the power and ability to choose which character you pay attention to, only you can prevent the Inner Goddess from going under. Have confidence and faith in your ability to steer your vessel, and don't worry about going off course. Always remember that *'you cannot alter the direction of the wind but you can always adjust your sails'* Keep Chitter Chatter and Fear at bay and just trust in yourself to stay afloat.

With less resistance, you are then able to absorb the Universal energy, the energy from the sun and the moon. You can programme your Internal Sat Nav (your Inner Goddess) so that she takes you to where you want to go, i.e you can work in harmony with the Law of Attraction, and simply glide through life almost as if on auto pilot. All of that rowing against the current, all of that drama – those days are over! Why would you choose to have it any other way? Just sit back and enjoy the amazing adventure on the Ocean of life, because it would be a terrible tragedy for you to miss it. This is your life – it is not a dress rehearsal. This is it, so grab it by the balls and shake it around a little bit.

Before we move on, I want you to relax, and think about where you would like your Inner Goddess to take you? You can be as realistic or as elaborate as you desire. There are no limits to manifesting dreams, so get it all out there. Then, if you are ready to truly begin to see real results, you can start to play around with programming your Inner Goddess and see where she takes you. If you find yourself not getting the results that you truly desire, then look again at your faith and belief. You must have 100% faith in your Inner Goddess before she will perform to her best ability. Stating your desires in the written format, is a habit to get into, as it clearly states what your current goals are.

'State it, visualise it, feel it, set it free, and watch as your life unfolds.'

So, being totally honest with yourself, and no holding back, list the top 10 things that you wish to come true in your life.

1 get rid of unnecessary anxiety

2 Life be easier finically

3 have more confidence

4 have the ability to believe in myself more.

5 stop worrying about things as much

6 stop trying to control things and 'go with the flow'.

7 Relax more

8 Be more impulsive

9 Be rid of my fear of flying

10 stand up for myself more

Now, you may even want to write down a copy of this list, and stick it someplace like your fridge, mirror, computer screen. Allow your subconscious mind to 'drink in' the contents, so that your Inner Goddess becomes very clear about what your life goals and intentions are. Remember: that when you feed the mind with information, it is sent deep into the subconscious, and this is the nerve centre that drives the Sat nav/ Inner Goddess. However, in order for the Sat Nav to actually drive with passion and high energy, we need to throw in a generous serving of 'feeling' into the equation.

Feelings are what truly set the wheels of the law of attraction in motion.

'what you think, you feel – and what you feel is what the law of attraction reads as being 'what you want more of'. '

What are you *feeling* right now? Not 'thinking'. But feeling – I want you to listen to your Inner Goddess right now, as she is the one who tells you how you are feeling. She communicates to you through physical sensations maybe? If I pause right now, I realise that I am feeling tense. I feel a knot in my stomach and my head is a little achy. Now, if I break it down and think logically about *why* I am feeling this way, I realise that it is because I have set myself the unrealistic target of getting another thousand words done on this book before I can go to bed. I just so happen to be really tired, and so this has caused me to put added pressure on myself, which in turn, has given me the dreaded 'writer's block' and... you get the idea!

But what was it that I could have done differently in the above process?

Was it that I set a thousand words as my new deadline? Not really. If I had been positive and had just effortlessly written the next thousand words then I would probably have slipped into what I call my 'zone' and my issue then would have been knowing when to stop writing and get some much needed sleep. My fall-down, was the moment that I began to panic about getting my writing done, Fear (here she is again!) crept in, doubt and panic set in and this in turn created a set of physical sensations as my Inner Goddess began to battle with fear and panic, and take control again before I would move into the next phase, that would be to adopt the role of the Victim.

Are you starting to see how the relationship between these little 'characters' work now?

The Vixen must listen to her Inner Goddess for warning signs as to when her feelings are off kilter, because if it goes un-noticed, you can bet your bottom dollar that pretty soon, chitter chatter, fear, panic, and a whole host of other feelings will soon invade the Vixen like a cancer, and this will give rise to the re-emergence of the Victim.

Let's continue the above situation that I was in just a moment ago to highlight that.

If I had continued to sit and stress over the fact that I had developed writers block (the one thing that I fear the most when writing!) then I would have found my head space going blanker by the minute and I probably would have moved rapidly from feeling panic and fear and 'what if..' . 'What if I can't find the words?' 'What if I can't ever find the words?' 'What if the book isn't done on time?' 'What if all that I am writing is terrible and will help nobody?' 'Why am I even writing this book?' Do you see the sort of mindset that these thoughts would be creating? Self defeat, doubt, a lack of self belief, a lack of self confidence, and again panic and Fear. I would spend so long fretting that of course, would not meet my self set deadline, and would most likely go to bed feeling like a total failure.

I would be going to bed, feeling like a Victim. But this would be my *choice* .

'the only thing that I would be a Victim of – is my own self created drama. Listening to my chitter chatter, listening to my fear, and NOT listening to my Inner Goddess'.

So: in order to be in the drivers seat in regard to our feelings, we need to become more aware of the kind of thoughts that we are feeding into our subconscious mind. Because this is what generates our deeper layer of emotions, and promotes this physical response/reaction.

Choose to battle, on a daily basis (yes, it takes a daily, conscious effort to put this book into action), Fear.

Choose to refuse to take on the Victim role ever again! If and when you see yourself sliding all too comfortably into that role, snap yourself out of it, and become aware of what you are thinking and feeling in that given moment. You can even write it down like I did above. Break it down, and look at firstly 1) your physical feelings 2) how and why did they come about? Look at the entire process, and then ask yourself 'are you handling this moment in the role of the Victim, the Vixen, and are you listening at all to your Inner Goddess?'

Not only is it vital to keep a check on your thoughts-feelings, for your own health and well being (and subsequent actions), your thoughts and feelings also have the incredible power to work in synergy with the Universe and the Law of Attraction in order to help create your reality.

'be the mistress of your own destiny – create your own reality. Your thoughts become feelings, your feelings guide you and the law of attraction responds, bringing you more of what you feel, because YOU are just like a magnet!'

THE RELATIONSHIP BETWEEN FEELINGS, YOUR INNER GODDESS AND THE UNIVERSE

Loving crack of the whip #7: *At any given moment, you can give in to the flow and simply just 'be'. Once you allow yourself to do this, life becomes almost effortless. Give yourself permission to be happy. Stop making life more difficult than it needs to be. The Universe is designed and waiting to deliver everything that is most suited to YOU. But how can it know what those things are when you aren't clear about it even to yourself?*

Once you stop choosing to play the role of the Victim, and do your best, on a daily basis, to drown out the sound of her and her buddies, chitter chatter and fear – your life will become based around the relationship between yourself (The Vixen) and the Inner Goddess (your inner voice/true you/intuition).

With the freedom that comes with this lighter, more positive load, also comes the opportunity to create the life that until now, you have only dreamt about.

Sounds cheesy right? And you're probably thinking 'oh the life that I have only dreamt about? You mean something completely unattainable and out of reach'. Well, yes and no. Of course, there are limits to getting certain things in your life. For example, when it comes to people. You are not going to attract and marry Brad Pitt whilst he is together with Angelina

Jolie, though I never like to say 'never' so if you do prove me wrong, I welcome your story!

But you can give it your best shot in other areas, and you won't like what I am about to say, but the only person responsible for you being exactly where you are in life, right now, is YOU. Your thoughts, your feelings, your listening to or not listening to your Inner Goddess, has brought you to exactly where you are today. Sure, there will have been things that were out of your control, that happened along the way. But remembering that you 'cannot alter the direction of the wind, but you can always adjust your sails', you will now have the knowledge that it does not matter what crap life throws at you, you can choose how you respond and act towards it.

'Don't forget – you always have the power and choice, to take a step back, and then act, rather than react'

Always take a step back, and give yourself the space and time in which to assess who it is that is speaking to you. Is it chitter chatter, fear, the Victim, or is it your Inner Goddess?

If you *have* been trying to listen to your Inner Goddess, your intuition, but somehow still end up in a place you'd rather not be, then this is okay! I am not saying that when following your Inner Goddess, life will be an effortless ride to perfection. Remember,that perfection is often simply a mirage, hiding the truth of reality. If you end up in a sticky situation but have followed your intuition, then you know that you are exactly where you should be and that life just has something in store for you, that you cannot yet see. But the main point that I want to reconfirm here, is that we are not looking to land up in a place of perfection, we are simply attempting to face up to accepting personal responsibility for where we wind up. We got us there, and we shall cope with things. There is no hiding behind the role of the Victim. Because a Vixen in tune with her Inner Goddess knows, that if she ends up in a stormy place as a result of following her Inner Goddess, all will be just fine because we can *always adjust our sails* accordingly and find a way to deal with absolutely anything. And yes, that may even mean admitting that there is no solution to something! But do you see the difference – trying, taking responsibility, and coming to that conclusion yourself, is totally different to sitting back, drowning in chitter chatter and fear and siding with the Victim, saying 'well what can I do?'.

A Vixen in tune with her Inner Goddess can be at peace with being in life's stormy waters. She acknowledges that it is just a part of the journey and with the adjustment of her sails, flows continually on the Ocean of life – failure and the words 'I quit!' are not an option. In the rather fabulous film 'Kinky boots', the leading character Charlie, is fed up of saying 'what can I do?' and grabs life by the balls, takes an alternative route with his father's shoe factory that has been left to him in his will, and decides to create women's boots for 'men', despite the risk that it entails. Losing his girlfriend in the process, he risks his home and love, and finds himself on the catwalk of the Milan fashion show in just his underpants and a pair of Northampton's finest! Life was not black and white, and he didn't just glide from A to B. But he listened to his inner voice, and just knew that he would get to where he wanted to go, even if he was not yet sure exactly where that location was!

My point in telling you the tale of Charlie from Northampton, is that he didn't just sit back, throw his hands up in the air and say 'well what can I do?'

'but what can I do?'

I of course can't and won't answer that! What YOU can do, is something that has to come from within YOU. That's my point! Listen less to chitter chatter, fear, and those around you, and work from the inside out!

But unless you shed your old skin, your outdated ways of thinking, that quite frankly, considering that you bought and are reading this book, you can't feel are working for you – you'll never know.

Throw yourself into the Ocean of life, and give yourself a chance to find out!

And p.s: you can actually do a lot more than you are maybe currently aware of, and so let's move onto the link between your Inner Goddess and the Law of Attraction.

Just before moving on, spend a little moment with yourself and list five things that you would do, if you could do them. What five changes would you make in your life / use the law of attraction to help you manifest?

1 Travel more

2 Stop worrying about what People think of me.

3 be happy with what i have

4 go on holidays abroad with

5 go on girlie nights out with old mends stuff.

Note: here, you have most likely listed things in the future tense, I would, I would like and so on. When we come to putting the Law of Attraction into practise further in the book, I will explain how the trick to changing a wish from being inactive, to active, is to state it in the present moment, as though it were already happening. For example, I have lots of money, I have a wonderful lover, I live in a fantastic new york style apartment. The secret is to really feel it, visualise and then it will begin to manifest into your reality. But totally feeling it, letting it absorb you can only really happen when you let go of Fear and dive right into the moment. Let's move onto this in a little more detail, as we look at the relationship between the Inner Goddess and the Law of Attraction and why we need to set ourselves free from the Victim in order for this stuff to *really* happen.

INNER GODDESS AND THE LAW OF ATTRACTION

I dream my painting and then I paint my dream – Vincent Van Gough

I don't want to delve too deeply into the complexities of the Law of Attraction, because that is a book in itself, and besides, there are some fantastic books already on the market that deserve accreditation and are definitely worth adding to your Goddess collection of essentials. You have probably heard of the book called 'The Secret' by Rhonda Byrne, and the Abraham Hicks book, 'Ask and it is given' by Esther and Jerry Hicks, is another great classic. I want to try and explain to you, the magic that can happen when you match your Inner Goddess to the energies of the Universe in a short summary, because this book aims to be practical, and so later on, in section two and three, I will continue to demonstrate how to begin to put the Law of Attraction into action. I don't want this book to be become another mind boggling, hard core, philosophical text book. I want you to get using the tools for transformation from day one.

I have already explained, how when you 'ask' it is 'given', and 'if it can be believed it can be conceived'. I have explained the relationship between our thoughts and feelings, and looked at how they work in harmony with Universal Energy, in order to bring more of what we think and feel back to us. This IS the Law of attraction.

The actual *theory* of the Law of Attraction is one thing, but since it was unleashed upon the world a few years back (although it dates back to the beginning of time) in the book 'The Secret', one of the main problems that people have reported, is the actual application of the techniques. If what we think and feel grows, then what happens when our old familiar faces chitter chatter, Fear and the Victim appear in our day to day life? Their ever whining presence, will surely bring more negative energy and emotion to us right?

I'd like to say no, but the answer to that question is YES. Luckily, the Law of Attraction does not jump on our *every* thought and feeling, you know, the little passing ones. I am not suggesting that you completely change your mindset and turn into this unrealistic robot, that never has any negative thoughts. That's just not human! But those consistent, general attitude thoughts and feelings do have an impact upon your reality. And it is those that we can alter, through doing *less* not more.

The more that you stress, worry, and over think who you should be, what you should be doing, the more you are listening to chitter chatter and Fear. The key to a fluid and happy existence, is to allow your heart, your soul, your Inner Goddess to guide you and lead the way. Just relax, and trust in your instinct a little more. Sure, it will feel unfamiliar at first, but baby steps become a mile and before you know it, you're well into your journey.

It is the habitual thoughts, the consistent thoughts, that create your mindset and your destiny... not the thoughts that come and go. The thoughts you consistently and continually plant into your unconscious become conviction in your life. You can use affirmation and meditation to do this, but making your new mindset a habit also takes discipline, commitment and resolve.

This is why the power of the will in your conscious mind is one of your greatest gifts. If you catch yourself in the middle of negative thinking, stop and say "No" to those thoughts. Stop the thought and replace it with a positive one. Either mentally or verbally, say "Cancel" and repeat your new thought. It sounds difficult, but it is easier than you think and becomes habit pretty quickly. In fact, once you truly grasp the concept that your consistent thoughts shape and determine your future, you find yourself almost effortlessly zapping any negative thought patterns away almost as if you are running on auto-pilot. And it is this 'running on auto pilot' , this sensation of almost 'gliding' through life that is where the magic happens. We have all had those days right? Where things just seem to fall into place. Your mind is not crowded by chitter chatter or fear, and rather than thinking in a million different directions all at once, you are almost 'thinking in a straight line'. Some would describe it like 'not thinking at all'. You just seem to know what needs to be done, what wants to be done, and you simply float from one thing to another, enjoying the beauty of the moment. This is the mind set that you want to try and create and attain.

So, if it is such a simple state of existence, who do so many people struggle to find this inner peace? If we have the key for our own ignition, then why do we struggle to turn ourselves on and set things to auto pilot? In a nutshell, we over think things. We complicate things. Less really is more and the only person who can gain this concept and find that clarity, is you, but the advice that I would give, is that you almost 'do not need to find inner peace, or gain that clarity' Practise the art of just 'being' and feed your mind with positive thoughts and intentions. In the words of Yoda **'do or do not, there is no try'.** Take the pure thought and set it free and allow the Universe and the law of attraction to act on it for you. Think it, know it, set it free, and that is all there is to it! Of course, this approach to life will take *some* effort on your part, as I said above. But it is the re-programming your mindset and creating the new habits that are the major part. The actual day to day implementation further down the line, will come to you as naturally as drinking water.

It takes 21 days to make or break a habit, and in this book, I will guide you through a 21 day programme to help you adapt to a new way of thinking (or not thinking – remember that less is more!) so that the role of the Vixen, and her Inner Goddess, become a natural essence of your day to day existence. How can it not come effortlessly, when it is after all, simply the emergence of the real you! The hardest part, will be the letting go of the security of the role of the Victim. But this, once you begin the process, is liberating.

'In setting yourself free, Unleashing your Inner Goddess, you are in the prime alignment, the optimum energy setting, to successfully activate the power of the law of attraction. '

You see – that is just it, the brick wall that most people face. The struggle between their Victim role, fear, chitter chatter, and their internal self. The background noise interferes with them being able to just 'be' and match their heartfelt desires to the Universal energy. And it is when you can do *this* that things really begin to transform.

This book is not only showing you how to adopt a new, stronger, more authentic role/self, it is also highlighting how once you grasp this concept, not only will you feel better instantly, more at peace – you will also find that the Universe begins to deliver things, people, experiences, travels, places, almost everything that you desire.

'It's like the buy one, get one free of the spiritual/self help world! Unleash your Inner Goddess, and not only will you become your authentic self, thus improving life and relationships, you will also set the wheels in motion for the Law of Attraction!'.

You see, once you stop talking yourself out of things, once you let go of Fear, and quieten your mind, YOU will emerge. Unleashing the real you, sets you free, to sail confidently on the Ocean of life. Using your Inner Sat Nav (the Goddess!), you can navigate your own route, in other words, you can work with the law of attraction, to go exactly to where you want to go. And if there are external events, and storms that are beyond your control, all will be okay, because you 'cannot alter the direction of the wind, but you can always adjust your sails', so you will come back stronger and more passionate, time after time!

This is just the beginning!

Let's now move into the 21 day programme, and look at how in just three little weeks, you can feel more energised, and refreshed, than if you took a three week vacation!

End of Section Summary
You choose to play the role of the Victim

There is no need to fear life – you cannot control the external events around you but you can choose how you react to them.

'You cannot alter the direction of the wind, but you can always adjust your sails'

- *With this in mind, why not make the choice to be the Vixen (you on a good day, (the authentic you) who is guided by her Inner Goddess?*
- *Listening to your Inner Goddess means that you will stay on your true life path*
- *You can also programme your Inner Goddess to take you to where you want to go in life.*
- *'What you think/feel, becomes your reality' so work with your Inner Goddess to create your own future. Connect to the Law of Attraction*
- *Your Inner Goddess is not only your Inner Voice, it is made up of 'energy'. You can step into the flow of giving and receiving energy, with others and also the Universe in order to nourish your Inner Goddess and those around you.*
- *You can utilise the natural Universal energies of the Sun and Moon in order to keep your personal energy recharged and this will be demonstrated further in the book via exercises.*

section two

Unleash your Inner Goddess

from Victim to Vixen

WHY 21 DAYS?

Maxwell Maltz introduced the theory that it takes 21 days to make or break a habit into the field of psychology and he has proven to be one of the most important authors in this field in the last 50 years. He recommends that a person should work on one area that they want to change at a time. The 21 day programme that I have designed for you focuses on 'improving your self image'. Until you change how you see yourself, and re-programme your subconscious to think and feel like a Vixen ,you will find it harder to keep the Victim and Fear at bay. There are numerous exercises that I guide you through over the course of the three weeks, but the main tool that forms the basis of this programme is the 'Goddess Vision board'. This is what does the hard work (you simply 'drink it in') and is used from day one/two onwards. You can implement the tools and techniques that I teach you and adapt them for other areas of your life that you want to improve once these 21 days are up.

Mission: to break the habit of listening to chitter chatter, fear, others – to stop choosing to play the role of the Victim. To get into the new and improved habit of thinking with clarity, confidence and passion about yourself and life – to kick ass as a Vixen who is in touch with her Inner Goddess, and who allows her Inner Goddess to guide her on the journey of life.

Before we begin, I want you to understand that there are no rights and wrongs when adopting the Inner Goddess philosophy/way of thinking. The ideas in this book are just a guideline, but the main thing that I am trying to encourage, is that you realise that less really is more. I am not a huge fan of hard work and bags of change in order to find yourself. You have always been there, you just lost sight of you along the way. Unleashing your Inner Goddess should not be complicated or difficult. You can embrace your inner self in whatever way you feel comfortable with, and live safe in the knowledge, that *your* way is always the right way for you, as you know yourself better than anybody. I am just here to try and help you see things with clarity, and take the first steps on this journey with elegance and ease.

'At all times choose to walk the path of least resistance'

The 21 day programme
The programme is designed to fit into or around your own schedule. Again, the advice that I give , is for you to take it and use it in the way that best suits YOU.

The 21 days have been divided into weeks for convenience, and techniques from week one, can also be used in week two, and week two in week three and so on. The idea is that you evolve during the 21 days and the exercises are timeless and once this programme has finished, you can continue to use them.

There is some effort involved on your part, and there will be some materials that need to be created. I have designed the programme so that you do the majority of the preparation, and the main exercises at the weekend. Then, for the rest of the week, you follow a routine, that incorporates morning and evening tools and techniques, using any materials that you have created, and focusing heavily on reprogramming your subconscious mind.

Again, I keep the routine adaptable, and at a length of time that should not interfere too much with your daily life. Why? Because it can be all too easy for the novelty of following a programme to wear off after just a few days, and I want this to be something that YOU stick to. I explain the morning and evening routines right after the weekend tasks, so you can even read up on what needs to be done for the coming week, before it arrives. That way, you do not need to feel like you have to keep referring back to a 'plan' that you have to follow, you can just absorb my information and slot it into your schedule when you feel ready to give it a go.

Most exercises will take around 15 minutes to complete, and the evening exercise has been designed so that you can even carry it out, as you relax in bed, before dropping off to sleep! The tools and techniques that I use, are simple but extremely effective, and the idea is, that once the 21 days are up, you will be so used to incorporating them, that they really will have become a habit, and you will stick to them on a long term basis.

Don't worry if you cannot do something, and don't 'try too hard'. The more relaxed you are, the better the results. Above all, only commit yourself to the 21 day programme if and when YOU feel inspired and ready to do so. It is designed so that you have fun and feel fabulous, so do enjoy! On that note, let's move onto week one.

WEEK ONE

Welcome to week one of the Unleash Your Inner Goddess Programme!

MISSION: To cleanse away the past and allow your Inner Goddess to breathe. To 'meet your Inner Goddess' and look at how to begin to look forwards from this new perspective. To lay the foundations of a new way of living.

This week we will look at the following: Meet your Inner Goddess, Drop your baggage at the door, Let's zap the Victim, Looking forward and not back.

Tools and techniques include: Cleansing the Vixen, Goddess make over and photo shoot, Goddess Vision Board (a staple of the 21 day programme), Write your own script

Weekend: You will carry out the larger exercises at the weekend and will also create your materials that will be used during the week. I have tried to work it this way so that those of you who have work or family commitments during the week, can slot this around and into your schedule.

Weekdays: You will carry out short exercises, tools and techniques every morning and evening, I have tried to keep the time slot to around 15-20 minutes for your convenience. The idea is, that the routines become a habit and over the 21 day period, alters your way of how you view and relate to yourself for the better.

You will need the following:
- *Olive Oil*
- *Sea Salt*
- *Lavender Oil*
- *A camera*
- *A red or pink candle and a white candle*
- *A cork board or cardboard for creating your Vision Board*
- *scissors, glue*
- *The outfit that makes you feel incredibly fabulous and sexy, make-up, basically, things for a photo shoot!*
- *An open mind*

Are you ready? Then let us begin....

Listening to your inner voice, your Inner Goddess, should always come effortlessly. When things feel uncomfortable (like a knot in your stomach) this is usually a good indicator that something is off. Physical sensations are a great way to know when your Inner Goddess is communicating with you, so listen to your bodies language. Choose the path of least resistance and when you feel resistance, ask yourself what your Inner Goddess is trying to tell you.

Now, before we continue, I want to do a little exercise with you that will help you truly connect/bond with your Inner Goddess.

It is all very well for me to talk about this Inner Goddess – but I do appreciate that some of you may be so wrapped up in depression, and self hatred even, that me just talking about her existence, is not enough to help you truly connect with her. So, I am going to get you to almost 'detach' yourself from your Inner Goddess for just a moment, so that you can meet her as though you were being introduced to an old friend.

It may be helpful for you to make notes, or even draw your Goddess, so I have included a space at the end of the exercise where you can get creative.

Meet your Inner Goddess!

A good technique that will help you access your Inner Goddess whenever you feel that you are maybe losing sight of her, is to visualise her as a little cartoon character, that lives deep inside of you. I'm not talking creepy, alien like inside of you – but just a magical spirit that exists in your essence. To make it easier, I am going to describe to you, my Inner Goddess

'I like to imagine that my Inner Goddess looks like Betty Boop. She is dressed in a red polka dot dress, and on her feet are shiny red kitten heels. She stands tall, and oozes sex appeal. She is confident, sassy, raw, but feminine. She is full of charm, warmth, humour and love. Like a star in the night sky, she twinkles day and night. She speaks from the heart, so is a true force to be reckoned with. her laughter is contagious and her smile illuminating.' Like the character that she resembles, I like to call her 'Betty'.

Now, close your eyes, and let your imagination run wild. What does your Inner Goddess character look like? Don't focus too hard on this visualisation. The first thing that comes into your head is her talking directly to you. Now quickly, almost as if in a stream of consciousness, let your mind pour its contents out into the space below. Describe what your Goddess looks like, acts like, sounds like, dresses like, and last but not least, give your Goddess a name.

> My goddess is strong confident
> fights fire with fire,
> Long flowing dark hair
> green eyes
> Fiery
> Passionate
> Funny

This may feel 'childish' but in the future, on dark days when you feel like you are disconnected from your Goddess, it is much easier to quickly access her, and magic her into existence, if you can visualise her rather than think in words. Besides, a little humour has never harmed anyone. If you have enjoyed this exercise, and are comfortable with being a little creative, you may even want to draw your Inner Goddess. I am no artist, so I printed off a picture of Betty Boop and keep it where I can see it daily, as a little reminder to communicate with Betty daily.

Personalising your Goddess, also makes her appear more like your closest Alie, an addition to yourself, your internal best friend. It reminds you that you are never quite alone, and you always have back up. Let's face it, on our lowest days, when we lose sight of who we really are and cannot see the wood for the trees, it is near enough impossible to dig deep within our soul and retrieve this 'Inner Goddess'. So being able to imagine that you are calling upon your secret superhero, means that even in your darkest hour, she is there in the wings waiting, and all you have to do is close your eyes and see her.

Picturing the Goddess as a small, feisty, separate entity also reminds you, that you are the Vixen, and the Inner Goddess is a part of you. She can exist within you, and when you call upon her to communicate with her, you can imagine her maybe sitting in front of you, on your shoulder when you need confidence, whatever makes you feel protected.

So – now that you have 'met' and befriended your Goddess, it's time to make a promise to yourself, but more importantly to her. Close your eyes and visualise her, and then talk to her. You can do this at any time, but right now, our aim is to acknowledge her feelings of having being ignored for so many years, and apologise to her, promise that from this day forth, you will make time to talk to her throughout each and every day.

A fun thing to do, is to create your own 'Inner Goddess' contract, that is between the Vixen (yourself) and your Inner Goddess. I have included a sample below, and you can fill this one in here, or even create a larger one, that you can then keep handy, as daily reminder of your goals/intention.

INNER GODDESS CONTRACT

Between the Vixen ....

and her Inner Goddess ....

Dated: ....

I .... vow to

communicate daily with my Inner Goddess.

I will listen to her above anyone else. I will turn to her when I

need advice. I will trust in her knowledge 100%.

I vow to keep up the battle between my Goddess and

her enemy The Victim,

and protect her from chitter chatter and Fear.

Signed ....

Again, you can print this off if you like, and keep it pinned to your fridge freezer, or close to your workspace as a gentle and loving reminder, that the most important change that you are going to make over the next 21 days (and beyond), is to acknowledge, listen to and communicate with your Inner Goddess.

DROP YOUR BAGGAGE AT THE DOOR

Loving crack of the whip #10: *Carrying around baggage does not make you a heroine. it simply tires you out, and makes you look like a Victim. You cannot change the past. But you can change the present, and this in turn changes your future. You cannot change events that happened to you or were inflicted upon you – but you can stop giving them the power to smother your Inner Goddess!*

'The Secret of health for both mind and body, is not to mourn the past, not to worry about the future, not to anticipate troubles, but to live the present moment, wisely and earnestly' Buddha

I have mentioned the idea of 'dropping your baggage at the door' several times so far, throughout this book. I now want to look at what I mean in a little more detail.

Firstly, we will discuss, what we think the word *baggage* refers to.

'Think of your memories of events that have left emotional scars, as your baggage. Like an overweight backpack, you carry them around daily.'

The straps begin to dig into your shoulders, your muscles ache, you stoop, don't stand straight, and find it hard to look people in the eye. No matter what you try to do to distract yourself from your baggage, over time, it becomes unavoidable and unbearable. Unless you shake it off, it will eat away at your spirit, until you are a shadow of your former self. Unable to jump forward into new and exciting life situations, the baggage makes spontaneity almost unthinkable. Not only because of the weight of it, but because the actual content of the baggage includes *Fear.*

Now if we go back to our theory that Fear can only have a place in our life if and when we allow it to, what happens to the baggage? It immediately lightens. Fear is the main emotion that gives power to the baggage that we carry.

Let's unpack your baggage!
If you visualise your baggage as being the backpack that I described above. Take it off your back, slowly, and place it on the floor in front of you. Imagine that you slowly open the top flap, and pull open the toggles, so that you can clearly see the contents.

Now actually imagine that this baggage, *has* been carried around for all of those years with you, through rain or shine, just imagine the stench that would come from exposing it to the daylight. There would be all manner of things festering! It is exactly the same for emotional baggage. Unless it is dealt with and aired, it rots away and becomes toxic, and if and when it is finally exposed (usually after a few gin and tonics, right?) it poses all kinds of problems and threats, not only to yourself, but to those close to you. Nothing good can come from it.

So why is it that we simply accept that this is something that we must do? Our cross to bear.

Take a moment to just jot down ten things that you may find in your backpack of 'emotional baggage'. These things can be actual life events, such as death of a parent, divorce, miscarriage, losing a job, personal 'failure' of some sort. Then, next to the event, I want you to think of an adjective that describes best, the emotion that you have attached to that event. For example:

- **break up of a relationship: fear** *of loving again and having my heart broken*
- **miscarriage: guilt** *that maybe somehow, it was my fault*
- **loss of a parent: guilt** *that I never did enough or fear of being alone*

These are just several examples, and yours will be applicable to you, but notice how guilt and fear feature so highly? Is it the same for you too?

Now, going back to what we have established in terms of Fear (and guilt) and how this holds us back, and keeps us stuck too-ing and fro-ing between the roles of Vixen and Victim – isn't this all that carrying this baggage around does? Let's be brutally honest here, carrying our burden does not benefit anyone else. In fact, how many relationships do you know of , or have been part of, that have suffered, maybe even broken down, because they could not stand the weight of yours (or the other parties) issues and baggage?

'When you allow your baggage to weigh you down, hold you back, feed fear and in turn give rise and power

to the Victim, you are denying your Inner Goddess the right to existence. You are only ever living your life to a fraction of your potential. You are throwing away talent, opportunities, you are denying yourself the right to you!'

In carrying baggage around with us, we are prolonging the original situation. We are choosing to keep our self stuck.

I know that this bold statement will provoke a reaction in many of you. How do I know this? Well, my life has had more than its fair share of ups and downs, heartache and pain. I had to go right to the bottom several times over, before I finally looked at myself in the mirror and vowed that it was time for change. And no, I don't mean 'changing myself'. But I 'woke up' and finally realised that the longer that I clung onto my baggage and used it as a reason, an excuse, a validation for my own confusing behaviour – the longer that the cycle would continue. I could not change the past, but I could make a difference to my present, and in turn, my future. I could take control of my own destiny, and not allow the past to control me for a moment longer.

It's not about forgetting some of the awful things that have happened to you. Because yes, some of those, may have been inflicted upon you, as a child, or by an abusive partner for example. The death of someone close to you, is not something that you can ever just 'get over'. But let's look at what exactly we mean by 'get over it'…

'Get over it' is a phrase that I really do not like. It is insulting in many situations. I prefer to look at things

with more of a 'whatever life throws at you, you take with you, as a part of you, but you grow from it' sort of attitude.

Everything that happens to you in life, is in some way, absorbed – **subconsciously**, via your conscious mind. It becomes a part of your history, your make-up. To just 'get over it' suggests repressing your feelings, sweeping things under the carpet and giving it the 'I am strong, things will not affect me' attitude. But is this sort of persona actually 'strong' ? Or is it a state of denial?

I am not going to answer that, because I want you to question things and form your own opinion.

LET'S ZAP THE VICTIM!

Before you do your Goddess photo shoot (that is done simply by YOU), we are going to look at an old Hoodoo tradition of 'ritual cleansing' of the physical self. It symbolises your readiness to almost shed your old skin (Victim) and neutralise any negative energy that may surround you. Not only can a cleansing be used for just that – cleansing – it can also incorporate some form of 'protection' using herbs or oils, so that you are safe guarded as you slide effortlessly into your new yet original persona.

Those of you comfortable with 'magick' may like to throw in a little protection or positivity spell. Maybe even a love spell, to encourage a deeper sense of self love and acceptance. But I don't really want to get into 'magick' talk in too much detail, as this book is designed to appeal to the individual.

Ideally performed in the evening, and again, when you are alone and able to get some space within which you can truly let yourself go, you will gather together the following items:

Goddess cleansing/bathing Experience!
- *Sea Salt*
- *Olive Oil*
- *Lavender oil*
- *A white candle and a pink candle.*

Run yourself a bath, or shower if you're more comfortable with that, and if you are in the bath, add 5 drops of Lavender oil into the water. (In the shower you can just drop them onto the floor so that they disperse and fill the cubicle with its relaxing infusion). Lavender is not only calming, it is also cleansing and protecting. It is a wonderfully healing oil that will remove any negative fears or worries that you may be presently caught up in. Allow yourself to completely relax, and visualise in your minds eye, your Victim energy dispersing, and disappearing into the water or down the plug hole. Take some sea salt (cleansing and purifying and used in past times for keeping away evil), and mix it with a little olive oil, and use this as a home made body scrub, to scrub away your former unrealistic self image in preparation for your new one.

Once you feel that you have cleansed away your Victim, dry yourself off, and then when you are relaxed and warm, light both of the candles (please assert caution when using naked flames). Place them in-front of you,and just sit and relax,allow yourself to 'drink in' the flame. Become lost in the flicker of the flame, go into a trance like state, and visualise the you who awaits for your Goddess photo shoot. Listen to your Inner Goddess, what is she wearing, what is her hair like? Maybe she is even naked – remember that this is for you to do whatever makes you feel most Goddess like, and is between you and yourself only.

The Goddess photo shoot!
This the moment where I say 'Gok Wan, eat your heart out'! If you are in the UK, you will most likely have seen a programme called 'How to look good naked'. This is where Gok Wan (stylist and Guru) helps a woman see herself as she really is, in

her all her glory, and celebrate her body by posing naked (tastefully) for the camera. Don't worry, nakedness is optional here, and the only person who is going to witness this shoot is YOU (unless of course you do have an exhibitionist side). The point of this exercise, is to create a photograph that captures the true essence of you, in all your feminine glory. For some of you, that may be daring to do a naked photo shoot. For others, it can be posing for the camera dressed up in that dress that really makes you feel Vamp like, or the secret underwear that you save for special occasions. But this is not about creating what you think sexy *should* be.

Let me tell you a little story. I once had a date, and I decided to pull out all the stops. My friend offered to come over, and help me 'do myself up' as she put it. Two hours later and I was looking like a drag queen slash hooker, and spent most of the night scared to breathe, for fear of popping buttons! I most certainly did not look like 'a better version of myself' and it's no wonder that the guy didn't call again. In all honesty, I look fabulous in fishnets and boots, and that is what I would wear for my Goddess shoot. But I can also feel equally sexy in jeans, flip flops and no makeup.

'Sexiness is an attitude. It originates from your Inner Goddess. It is your Goddess expressing herself. Like a light that is switched on, sexiness radiates and attracts others like moths to a flame.'

If you don't *feel* sexy then it won't be oozing from your every pore. Sexiness is an attitude, and it is your signature individual appeal. There is no 'set format' for creating sex appeal. Only you can generate it within. So whether it be something that is stirred within you from a good bass line, or the soft flicker of candle light, a good way to go about starting to prepare for your shoot, is to surround yourself with things that create a certain atmosphere and mood for you.

I would light a few red candles, as these represent passion and self confidence, self love, passion and sex. I would feed myself cherries and strawberries, and sip Italian Prosecco. I may treat myself to a self applied massage, using homemade oil (base oil and a few drops of rose and ylang ylang as these are aphrodisiacs), I would then spend time applying my make up, creating a Vampish look, and I'd wear a simple black dress, with stockings and knee boots. *Underneath* this ensemble, I would maybe add my own secret signature, such as a garter, or hold up fishnets, with a suspender belt. There is something wonderful about hidden weapons, that only you are aware of. Have you ever tried wearing your most expensive, extravagant underwear underneath your work clothes for the day? If not, try it! Somehow, you feel powerful, Goddess like, and your whole body language changes. People around you know that something is different about you but they can't quite put their finger on it. It's similar to the school of thought of 'wearing heels with anything' – it instantly gives you that surge of confidence and you just stand tall and appear more feminine.

'Create your own look, this is about you exploring your sensual, sexual, classy, feminine side.'
If you feel Goddess like in a bin liner and sandals, then girlfriend, get it on! There is no 'ideal' image here. This is an expression of the Inner you, using tools such clothing, make-up almost like an artist uses a paintbrush and canvas. Create a masterpiece, and enjoy the entire process. Create an

ambiance, and lose yourself in the moment. Nobody else is going to see you doing this, this is entirely about you spending time with yourself, The Vixen having a girlie night in with her Inner Goddess, VIP access only.

Then it's lights! Camera! Action!

It may seem a little odd, doing a photo shoot *solo*. You are probably thinking 'yes, but how on earth do I get a decent picture? I can't fit the whole of me in, I need someone else here to hold the camera'... This is not about creating the perfect snap shot. It is not going to be shown to anyone, or posted on Facebook. (although if you love the outcome, then why the hell not?) The purpose of this, is to capture a moment.

'Relax, let go – and just snap away. Capture the essence of you, the moment. If you're laughing with your mouth open, fantastic! Or if you are posing like Angelina Jolie, give it your best pout! But the trick is, that when you are in the height of enjoyment, and you're really feeling comfortable, capture that!'

The primary focus of this exercise, is for you to enjoy the process and not the outcome.

Once you are happy that you have the shot that you want to go on your board, print it off, and keep it somewhere safe.. In the next exercise, you are going to create a 'Goddess Vision Board' and you will stick this photo right in the centre. Why? Well, on this board, you are going to create a collage of images, words, and ideas, that represent what the word 'Goddess' means to YOU. You will then stick this photo of yourself in the centre, and will be surrounded by all of that positive symbolism. When you create your Vision board, you will generate an intense 'feeling' and YOU will then be anchored to that. Do you see where I'm going with this? You are part of the emotion now, you are mingling with the Goddess club, and as your subconscious mind drinks this collage in, you are being absorbed with it.

Your subconscious mind, will slowly but surely begin to register the image of YOU as being associated with everything that you have chosen to represent the Goddess attributes. A shift will take place internally. The main aim of this book, is to promote this internal shift, to enable you to feel sexier, sassier, relaxed, vibrant, and in tune with your feminine self.

LOOKING FORWARDS AND NOT BACK!

Loving crack of the whip #11: *The past is gone: and the longer that you keep on looking back there, the longer that you will remain stuck with one toe in the pool of the Victim. A Vixen in tune with her Inner Goddess practises being present in this very moment for she knows that what she focuses on creates her future. Focusing on past pain simply keeps you attracting the memories. Only YOU can lovingly assert yourself into your future.*

Now, I want you to think about creating something known in the self help industry as a 'Vision board'. I have renamed this tool as a 'wishion board' as it embodies your vision (goals), but also a sprinkling of magic wishing! The purpose of a Vision Board, is to primarily enable your dreams, visions and desires, to embed themselves deep into your subconscious mind. Going back to the Law of attraction, vision boards are often used as a great tool for helping your dreams manifest into reality. As you are now aware, the law of attraction works, when your thoughts produce feelings, and this in turn generates an energy that is almost magnetic, that draws your desires to you like gold dust. But in order to generate the belief, that what you wish for is on its way to you, you need to get this belief right into your subconscious mind. One way of doing this is to practise daily affirmations, but I am not a huge fan of those. The problem with affirmations, can be that you are somehow detached from them. You stand at your mirror, repeating them almost robotically, but unless you are actually *feeling* the words, then you may as well be reciting Shakespeare.

The subconscious mind has a knack at 'drinking' in images and symbols. There is a form of 'Magick', known as Sigil Magick, and this relies upon the mind drinking in a symbol that has been crafted to incorporate a word or secret message. It is a simple but highly effective form of Magick, and the use of a Vision board works on the same principle. Your mind will absorb the message with the least effort – this truly is the path of least resistance.

So, let's create your Vision/Wishion Board!
What you will need:

- *A cork board. You can usually get them from discount stores or £ and $ shops.*
- *Pins*
- *Or if you prefer: a cardboard cut out board, that you will glue your images onto.*
- *A selection of images as outlined below.*
- *An open and honest mind*

Okay, so the actual creating a Vision board is not in the least bit complicated, and should only take around 10-15 minutes to complete. Like I said, I want to make this journey as stress free and easy as possible, but for the techniques that I will give you to be highly effective and be something that you can continue to incorporate into your daily habitual routine on a long term basis.

The *difficult* part (for want of a better word, it is only as difficult as you make it) is letting your imagination run wild, and being completely honest with yourself about what you want to go onto your Vision board.

So, what exactly does go onto this board? The idea is, that you find photos, pictures, words, anything you like, that represents the general image that you are trying to build. In regular boards used solely for general purposes in the study of the law of attraction, individuals will usually stick photos that represent things such as: their ideal partner, their dream house, their fantasy sports car, love, money – the end result is a collage that stimulates an emotional response generated from the excitement attached to the possibility of seeing their dreams turn into reality. With a Goddess board, we want to create a collage that screams 'Goddess!' to us when we look at it. Now of course, what one of us finds Goddess like, another may not, and so this board will be entirely personal, between just you and yourself. So really let your imagination run riot. You can add a little sexiness into the mix if it gets you going, but the main goal is to really get you fired up!

My Vision board would include: Splashes of my favourite sensual colours, red, hot pink, purple and black. A dash of leopard print, and a little leather and lace. Images of Kitten heels, Fetish icon Bettie Paige, Dita Von Teese, Angelina Jolie and Madonna. Fishnet tights, black cocktail dress, thigh high boots, a whip, red lipstick'. You get the idea! Mine is a little edgy, verging on the erotic, because this is what personally gets me feeling aroused, and sensual. But yours must reflect your Inner personality. The trick is, to coax out your femininity, and tune into your Inner Goddess. As we are looking to harness the Goddess within, it would be a good idea to choose role models that you aspire to be like, and Goddess clothing that you only dream of wearing.

Then, once you have assembled your collage together, you are going to take the photo that you did on your Goddess photo shoot, ' and this will be pinned smack bang in the middle of this board. It will then be placed ideally in a location where you can see it before falling to sleep, and first thing upon waking.Of course, if you live with your partner then you can keep it inside your wardrobe, or under the bed, and just get it out and spend some time with it when you won't be disturbed. But you will need to work with the board every day, for the next 21 days, for at least 15 minutes a day.

An ideal state to get yourself into, when using the board, is what you may be familiar with as being a 'meditative state', or a trance like state, of deep relaxation. Don't look too hard at the images on the board, simply allow your eyes to flicker over them, drink them in, it should happen effortlessly. If you feel like you zone out and things become blurry, all the better. The less that you are 'consciously thinking' and are 'subconsciously drinking' in the board, the quicker that your desired Goddess persona will manifest into your reality, as an extension of your personality.

So next on the agenda, is to write your own script for how you now want life as a Goddess to be!

Write your own script

So, let's take a moment to pause and recap all that we have covered so far in terms of the 21 day programme. Remember, that this is not a 'set programme'. There are no rights and wrong, and this can take you as little or as long as is right for you to follow. The main philosophy is that you break free from the chains that bind you and have you limiting your self beliefs, and so the last thing that I want this book to do, is make you feel like you have to adhere to something or change your ways. You can use this book as suits you best.

So far you have:
- *Met and visualised your Inner Goddess*
- *Maybe you have even named her*
- *Signed a contract with your Inner Goddess*
- *Promised her and yourself, that you will have daily communication with her*
- *Cleansed yourself of your outdated self image and the Victim and acknowledged that on your clean slate you are in complete control of who and want you will be*
- *Enjoyed a fun and liberating private Goddess photo shoot.*
- *Created a Goddess Vision (wishion) board and defined what the term Goddess means to you and what and who inspires you to feel sexy, sensual, empowered and Goddess like.*
- *Put yourself at the centre of the Goddess Vision board – immersing yourself in the Goddess energy*
- *Have now started to utilise the board, placing it somewhere where you can see it daily, to allow it to work on your subconscious/self image*

So next, you are going to 'write your life script'

In order to make real changes, I believe that it is imperative that you set clear goals.

But again, I want you to unleash your Creative spirit, and write with passion and from the heart. I don't want you to think logically about what you can or cannot realistically achieve over the next year, five years, ten years and so on. A lot of 'self help' books do look at setting real goals that you will hopefully achieve, but the aim with this exercise is not to actually worry too much about meeting the goals, but to get your juices flowing in terms of inspiration, motivation, dreams and passions.

My list may look something like this:

I hope to publish a series of successful books that will inspire women worldwide. I will also hold Goddess workshops, and creative workshops, to encourage the freedom of choice, spirit and self expression. I intend to see as much of the world as possible before I die, and would love to settle in a beautiful Sicilian house, where I would write, walk, cook Italian food, and maybe spend time with a handsome soul mate who is also spiritual and passionate. Children would be perfect, as would a chocolate brown Labrador and shocking pink moped called Daisy.

I did not pause to think about what I wanted to appear on my script, and yes, mine is short and sweet. Yours can be as long and elaborate as you like. The idea is that you get lost in the moment, wander off into a daydream, and really visualise what/where you Goddess would like to be. Jot it all down and then leave it lying around somewhere where you can read it when you need a pick me up. Of course, if you share a place and don't want others to see such things, why not invest in a folder and keep everything together so that you can just pull it out and read it at home, at work, on the bus... you get the idea.

The fun part of this exercise, is looking back at the list a few years down the line. If you haven't even come close to your dreams being fulfilled then you will know that you have not truly been listening to your Inner Goddess.

Visualisation is a vital part of changing your destiny. There are many tools out there that encourage people to visualise the changes that they want to occur, then there are those that work on reprogramming the subconscious mind. But in order for it all to come together, you need to match your conscious mind with your subconscious mind. Active thoughts of the conscious mind add fuel to the subconscious mind and sets its wheels in motion. This then cultivates an emotional response in the form of feelings, and this is when you are at your most powerful , when you are emitting feelings and energy based upon the changes that you want to come about. The Law of Attraction will pick up on these and will take you down the road that leads you to such changes to come about. But that aside,on an immediate, personal level, just working on your mind in such a way, will change your feelings, and you will be operating from a higher state of confidence on a daily basis. This will have immediate effects upon your performance in all areas of your life, and if nothing else, you should start to feel happy and like a weight has been lifted.

Now that the weekend is over, and you have worked out how to free yourself from your past, and have defined who/what your most authentic self is – we can look at some things that you can do during week one in terms of short, but highly effective daily tools and techniques. The idea is that these can be slotted into even the busiest woman's daily life, so that this programme is do-able and realistic.

So: *here are your morning and evening exercises for week one, incorporating the materials that you have just created.*

A.M When you wake, ideally, the first thing that you will notice, will be your vision board. For just ten minutes, allow yourself to drink in the images on your board. This is the ideal state within which to do this, as your body and mind are still in a deep state of relaxation, so you will not be interrupting the absorption of the material, with thinking. Then, when you rise, start your day with a cup of hot water with lemon juice before you have any form of caffeine. I don't really want to look too much at diet in this book, as diet is a personal choice, and if you wanted a diet or detox book, you would have bought one of those instead. But I do want you to slot in just a few extras that I know will help you feel 'revitalised'. Hot water with lemon juice is one of them, and this is a fantastic boost to a sluggish system, it will cleanse your liver, kidneys, digestive system and skin, and will have you glowing by the end of the 21 day period, which all helps with confidence.

When you head to the bathroom, treat yourself to a cleansing ritual, like the one that you performed at the weekend. It does not have to be as lengthy, because I know that time is of the essence, when you may have to get to work, or get up and look after the children. So a simplified version of this, is to make up a little plastic bottle of cleanser (you can buy those empty plastic bottles for not very much at the drugstore, or you can even use an old bottle that you have at home). Simply add some olive oil to the bottle, and then some lavender oil (around 10 drops if a largish bottle, but there is no real measure on this, just determine it using your own sense of smell and personal preference). Then, add some sea salt, as this will naturally detoxify but also exfoliate. As you rub this all over your body, visualise scrubbing away your worries, your stress, your negativity, and most of all, your Victim and her friend fear. This will really clear your mind and start you off with a 'clean slate'.

Next, before you dress, I want you to spend just ten minutes applying a home made lotion, oil or powder. The choice is yours as to preference, and here are some ideas to get you started. I personally would take a base oil, or a base cream. You can buy these from aromatherapy shops, large chemists, and they are used for mixing with essential oils for massage. Then, to this base, I would add some oils of my choice. I don't really want to give you a fixed recipe because part of the fun of this is the choosing the oils that most suit your specific needs and taste. In the back of the book, I have included a run down of crystals, oils, and other ingredients to help you choose, but my personal example would be: Rose oil simply because I adore the smell, and it is a mood elevator, but is also used for attraction, romance and self confidence. Lavender (relaxation and protection), geranium (balancing).

Every morning, massage your potion into your skin, and visualise it as being a protective shield, that keeps fear and the Victim at bay, but works like a magnet to pull the Universal energy to you. Imagine that this potion actually helps activate the law of attraction, and also draws people to you. Once you are ready for the day, off you go, knowing that you can take on any challenge but remain in tune with your Inner Goddess.

P.M The evening is when you will be at your most creative and productive, because you have more time to relax and focus on getting lost in the moment. You can incorporate the idea of bathing ritual into your evening routine. Use your imagination and adapt it to best suit your own needs. Work it around the kind of day that you have had. If you feel run down, negative or have encountered your Victim, then do a cleansing ritual, but experiment with oils and crystals and candle light and create a bathing environment best suited to your mood. If you are not feeling very creative, here are some quick tips: white candle for purity, red or pink for self love and self confidence and drawing others to you. Rose quartz or clear quartz are the idea crystals for week one, to heal and build your self confidence and your relationship with your Inner Goddess. Rose, Lavender and Geranium oils are wonderful mixed with milk protein for a soothing and protective bathing experience.

In the bath, or if you prefer not to bathe daily, just use a candle and burn some oils, close your eyes, and visualise yourself emerging as your true self. What do you feel like, look like, and how is your life panning out? Think about the script that you wrote and how you would like your life to start to become. I say this, rather than 'how you would like your life to be' because I think that the problem with visualising the *future,* is that it can feel all too far away and it is easy to become disheartened. So in week one, just try and focus on yourself in the process of moving forwards and evolving. Your visualisations can be as simple as:

- *what will you wear tomorrow as a Vixen in tune with her Inner Goddess?*
- *How would you like your day to go? What will you produce/achieve/experience?*

In week one just quite simply visualise from day to day – only ever look as far ahead as the next day at the start of this process, so that you can get used to visualisations, and your goals are broken day into daily bite size chunks.

This week is about transformation and leaving your past behind, whilst taking the first steps into the warm ocean of your new life.

When you are in bed, you can spend time unwinding before sleep, looking at your Vision board again. If you take a long time dropping off to sleep, you may also like to visualise your transformation again, but this depends on what you prefer. You may benefit more from simply gazing at your vision board, as you feel your eyes closing over, and you begin to dream about the last thing that you have just seen.

These exercises are *simple* but *effective*, as they are all working on reprogramming how you feel about yourself, working on a *subconscious* level.

On a daily basis, through practising these short and simple steps, you will be gently reminding yourself about what you want from life, how you want to work alongside your Inner Goddess, and your battle to keep the Victim at bay. It may even seem a little too easy for some of you, and that's great! The idea of this book, is not to weigh you down with a load of fancy information, and confuse the hell out of you. It is to gently guide you back to your inner, most authentic self, to shine a light on what and who is already, and has always been present – YOURSELF.

WEEK TWO

Welcome to week two of the Unleash Your Inner Goddess Programme!

MISSION: With the clean slate that was laid in week one, we move forwards with creating a lifestyle fit for a Goddess!

This week we will look at the following: Out with the old and in with the new

Tools and techniques include: Goddess Clear out

Weekend: Goddess Clear out, What's your style?,

Weekdays: A.M and P.M routines

You will need the following:
- *Olive Oil*
- *A Red Candle*
- *A Red Lipstick or lip gloss*
- *Stockings*
- *Garter*

Weekend: Over the weekend you are going to treat yourself! No sitting at home creating tools – you are going to get out there, and live a little. I do of course understand, that you have personal commitments, families, partners, and a cash flow to take into consideration and so I am going to offer alternatives to the following exercises where applicable.

In week one, you looked at how your past had been keeping you stuck, and set out clear goals and desires, about letting go, cleansing yourself of your Victim, and redefining the way that saw yourself – how you saw yourself as a Vixen in tune with her Inner Goddess.

This week, we are going to think more about how to communicate and play with your Inner Goddess. Looking back and analysing our Victim self is not really applicable now. That time has gone, and today is a new beginning.

This weekend, you are going to indulge in the 'Goddess Clear out' and then get *creative!*

First however, I want us to think about *why* a clear out is good for the soul. Have you ever realised just how much influence, your external surroundings have on how you feel internally?

Your home, your wardrobe, your mode of transport – all of these material things are a reflection of your internal makeup. Of course, you may not like where you live right now and wish that you could change it. Yes, circumstance does have a huge part to play in all too. But make the most of what you do have, and put your mark on it.

When a person is depressed, they often let their surroundings and personal appearance go right? I know this applied to me when I suffered with clinical depression.

And I can just tell when someone is feeling great on the inside, because it somehow comes across in their hair, make-up, their appearance. We all have those days, when we don't feel so great on the inside, and we know that it reflects on the outside, same as we can be feeling perfectly fine on the inside, catch a glance at ourselves in the mirror, or go home to a messy apartment, and we quickly crumble internally.

Now, I am not saying that material possessions, places, and makeup and clothes are essential for inner peace and happiness. In an ideal world, we would be able to remain happy even if all of our hair and teeth fell out and we wore sack cloth and ashes. But the majority of us, do want to look well presented and healthy, as that is just a fact of modern day life.

Your Inner Goddess knows that she is fantastic without such things, but can be equally happy to play around with her personal space and appearance, simply because she can.

I am not about to start telling you that you should give away all of your possessions and become a spiritual recluse who focuses only on her internal connection and energy. The aim of this book, is to look at how to stay in tune with your Inner Goddess whilst also having a normal life in the modern day world. We have the gift of being in the position to be able to create with our home, appearance and choices/tastes, but now that you are looking at shedding your old skin *metaphorically*, maybe now is the time to think about having a good old clear out *literally*.

How would you like your Inner Goddess to be reflected and expressed via your external surroundings and appearance?

OUT WITH THE OLD AND IN WITH THE NEW!

Time for a Goddess clear out

Start off, by spending an hour looking through your closest, and your bathroom cabinet and make-up bag. You'd be amazed how much the way we take care of ourselves and dress can influence how we feel internally.

Bathroom: look at your products. Do you follow a decent skin care regime? If not, why not? It doesn't have to cost the earth, and you can even use natural ingredients from your very own kitchen to get yourself sparkling in no time at all! Did you know that Olive Oil makes an excellent cleanser? Simply warm a little oil in the palm of your hands and massage allover. Remove with warm water. It may leave a little residue, so how about toning with apple cyder vinegar? It removes brown spots, cures acne, and tones and firms the skin! On days when you fancy a little exfoliation, just add some sea salt to your olive oil, and buff away. I do recommend the purchase of a good moisturiser, that contains an spf however, as it's the only way to prevent ageing and skin cancer. Incorporate the Goddess pampering into your morning and evening routine, you can even use the oil on your face in the bath or shower, keep it simple. But as you complete your skin care regime, don't rush through it. Imagine that your face is a museum exhibit, a fine painted porcelain doll. Would you disrespect it and scrub away carelessly? No. Handle yourself with care and nurture yourself from the inside out.

Make-up bag: Treat yourself to a funky makeup bag, something that is Goddess like and fill it with your staple items. If you don't really wear much makeup, that's okay. But if you do, and you know what suits you, then gather your products together and spend a few minutes every morning this week, trying something different. I don't mean have a complete image overhaul, as this could e disastrous and the idea is not to change who you are. I don't want you to feel that you have to hide behind masses of make-up. But if for example you like to wear lip colour, try adding a top coat of lip plumping gloss. Or if you use clear mascara, try a little dark brown instead.

Closet: Have a good clear out ! This is the time to be ruthless and brutally honest with yourself. Make two piles –

Pile One: clothes that you wear regularly
Pile Two: Clothes that you have not worn for the last 6 months or more.

Simple: Pile one you keep, pile two goes to the nearest charity shop. No place for sentimentality, personal growth involves doing some things that make you feel a little uncomfortable.

Push your boundaries and enjoy it!

What is your personal style?

I want you to sum up, in just one word, how you would describe your personal style.

I would describe my personal style as ....

For example, if I had to choose one word, then I would describe my personal style as *Bohemian*. I do not follow fashion, or ever wear what I think I should be wearing, my choice in style reflects my attitude. But to what extent does the way that we dress on the outside, reflect who we are on the inside? Think about the following:

How have you felt if you have ever had to wear a Uniform? How would you feel, if we were all told by the government that we had to wear a bland uniform every day for the rest of our lives?

Have you ever placed yourself in a group (as a teen maybe) where clothing was part of your identity? For example, goth, rocker, rapper.

Do you think that the way that you dress *now* is in some way intended to express your personality?

Identity is a complex subject. There should be a relationship between how you feel on the inside and what you wear on the outside. Your style is an expression of your Inner Goddess in all her glory. And I am not talking about fashion, or choosing a particular trend to follow. Style is something individual. Style does not have to fit into a category or a box. It does not have to be defined. I know, that my style changes according to my mood. I have 'colour moods' (and colour also influences our state of mind), and so on. But I like to think of my internal self, and my external self as working together almost like 'Yin and Yang'. They need to work together in unity, or somehow, I just start to feel off kilter. So keeping this description in mind, if I am feeling unbalanced, one way of addressing this, could be to look at how I can influence my mood and state of mind by altering things around me.

It can also work the other way round, if I am feeling great internally, I can express this through my external surroundings and have a bit of fun with it.

Remember, that style does not define you. It is not who you are. Start inwards and work outwards – your style is simply a fun way to express your Inner Goddess, or to improve your mood, but you cannot work outwards and in. You will not find your Inner Goddess, the real you, in a pile of material, or cosmetics.

I also like to think of your style as being so much more than just certain types of clothes, shoes or bags. Have a minute, and just think about colours. What colours do you most often wear? Jot down the 3 most common colours that run through your wardrobe and also in your personal space

Then, next to each colour, write down an adjective that you feel best describes that colour, and look at whether or not it or not it applies to you.For example. I wear a lot of black, brown and red. Black is dark,brown is boring and red is sexual. If I am feeling down in the dumps, I often throw on a black ensemble. It is very rare that I am inspired to wear red, yet it happens to be one of my favourite colours. Why do you think this is? I can tell you why – I find that red attracts a lot of attention every time that I have worn it. It is afterall, the colour of sexual attraction and desire. But on days when I do not like myself all that much, why on earth would I want others on the street to notice me? To take myself out of my comfort zone, I try and push my boundaries, and wear a little red on the days that I don't feel so fabulous. Nothing too extravagant, it can be something as simple as accessorising a black outfit with a red brooch, or a red handbag., But colour is a fascinating mirror, to show us exactly what we are feeling. Have a think about what role colour plays in your life and how you can go about shaking things up a little.

So – when you have looked through your possessions, how much of it has reflected your former self, and the role of the Victim? Have you been guilty of any of the following things?:
- *holding onto clothes that are drab and do not even suit or fit you*
- *wearing clothes to hide yourself because you are lacking in confidence to show who you really are*
- *sticking to the same make-up and skincare routine that you have used since 16 because it feels safe*
- *storing clothes that you can no longer fit into just in case 'one day' you can again*
- *wearing things that you don't even really like, just because*

they are there and you feel guilty for shopping or treating yourself.

We have all been guilty of it at some time or other. So many women make do with hand me downs, or charity shop clothing that they buy, just because it was the cheapest thing that they could find. How often do you save a little aside and treat yourself to something new, just because you are worth it?

Even with shopping and fashion, many of us choose to play the role of the Victim and choose to continue to believe that we are somehow not worthy of looking and feeling fabulous.

Before moving onto the exercise for this weekend, I want to take a moment for us to think about the relationship between our Inner Goddess and how we present ourselves on the outside and via our image and surroundings. We can use our external image and surroundings as a gauge, to see whether or not we are feeling happy internally. I know, that when I am having a bad day, I don't make as much effort with my physical appearance, some days I don't even brush my hair or apply any make up, and my house can become unkempt, even messy. Do you have any physical manifestations that work in the same way? Jot them down below, and then from now on, if and when you notice these things spiralling out of control, you can regain control and try and work out what it is that is preventing you from feeling connected to your Inner Goddess.

Think of the relationship between your internal self and your external self as being similar to the Yin and Yang. There is a definite intrinsic relationship between the two. However, inner peace, comes when we can acknowledge this, but also clearly define between the two. Let me go into this a little deeper.

I have already looked at how we can use our exterior as a way to monitor what is going on internally. But it's not always that easy to define. Some women appear to be well presented at all times externally, so does this mean that they are in tune with their Inner Goddess daily? Sadly, not always. What YOU need to work out, is which category you fall into, and then from there, you can think about how your exterior works in tune with your Inner Goddess.

In today's society, a lot of women have become addicted to cosmetic enhancement. Breast augmentation, botox, surgery, collagen, hair extensions, nail extensions, eye lash extensions, spray on tan – the list is endless! But an awful lot of these women, admit that they turn to such enhancements in the pursuit of finding happiness. But the question we need to ask is

'can we rely upon our exterior to feed our interior? Or are we in pursuit of the impossible?'

We have all seen cases where the quest for the perfect face or body becomes an addiction, an obsession. There is always just one more procedure and then happiness will result – but it rarely does. So how can I be suggesting that you express your Inner Goddess through your creative exterior, yet look at how creativity with the body can also be a way to hide deep rooted insecurity? Well, the shift that needs to take place, is that you begin by looking at how you feel internally, and then from there, work on accessing your most authentic self. And then, and only then, can you know what you true image that reflects your Inner Goddess is going to be.

The key is to get a healthy balance and relationship between the exterior and interior – when you are in tune with your Inner Goddess, your energy will be at its optimum peak and you will be working in alignment with the Universal energy and the law of attraction. As a result, you will be drawing everything most suited to the authentic you, into your reality. You will have the inner confidence to wear whatever your intuition tells you to.

How many times have you put on the thing that your inner self wants to wear, but then taken it off, because the chitter chatter voices in your head convince you that you are too 'old, fat, ugly' to wear it? Be honest... I know, that when I was insecure, I would frequently get ready to go out, and then the thought of walking around simply to get the bus in heels with a skirt, made me panic. Panic – why? Well, more often than not, there was no *logical* explanation for the emotion running through my body. But my reasoning often went along the lines of 'I know I have a good body, and this skirt and these heels will draw attention from people because of that but then they will look up and see my face, and notice all of my flaws'. Now the flaws that I was convinced would make the general public sneer at me ranged from pre-menstrual acne, to what I considered to be a long nose. In my mind, I had totally convinced myself that I would come across as being someone who was attempting to look beautiful, but people would spot that I was a 'fake'.

Finally, after much soul searching years down the line, I established that what the actual problem was, was an internal belief that I was not good enough and I was looking for something externally to focus on and blame, thus avoiding looking at the deeper issues.Don't get me wrong, I'm not saying that there will always be 'deeper issues' – my dislike towards my acne was very real, and I know, that we really can just genuinely dislike something about our physical appearance to the point that it truly gets us down. But the body is transient. It changes over time and so in a way, we cannot ever totally rely upon it for our happiness or sense of identity. We have to find something stable within to identify with. For instance, what if you were in a horrific accident and lost the face that you once recognised as you? Would you completely lose all sense of who you are? No! So the relationship between the external and internal is complex – it does work concurrently yet where the exterior can be altered dramatically, fundamentally our interior remains constant, we just lose 'us' along the way through drowning in baggage and fear, to name just a couple of reasons.

Therefore, playing around with our external image can be a great creative outlet for expressing our Inner Goddess, and we can also know, on days when we are not taking the best care of our reflection, that there may be something else going on inside. But ultimately, we need to always be working from the inside out, and not look externally to find interior happiness and security.

Take a good and honest look at yourself as you stand today. Does your exterior reflect your interior? Whether you look 'amazing' or drab, both of these as we have discussed, can demonstrate a lack of confidence. I am not suggesting that in order to express your Inner Goddess, you look drop dead gorgeous every day. When I am most in tune with my Inner Goddess, I walk around barefoot, in jeans, with a clean and simple tight t.shirt. I let my hair hang loose and I wear little makeup. This is a personal and individual journey and only YOU can apply the questions that I raise to your own situation and experience.

The idea of this following exercise, is not that you go looking for what you *think* a Vixen in tune with her Inner Goddess should wear, but *you listen to where and what your Goddess guides you to.* If it is to the tight dress that you worry you're too big to wear in public, forget what *others* think and start to live your life for *yourself!* Or if you are used to masking yourself in a protective image that does not represent the real you, shed that skin and feel liberated by trying out the less is more approach.

So let's get out there and Unleash your Inner Goddess on the world of fashion and beauty!

For this exercise, you will need to take a photograph, so try and get hold of a camera or maybe a phone with an inbuilt camera.

Head into your local town, to the one shop that you would love to be able to buy all of your clothes from. The price of things in there is irrelevant, but we all have that one shop where we know that if we walk in, we will see plenty of items that we think would suit us.

Now, walk in, and allow your Inner Goddess to guide you. The thing that you are most drawn to, go right over, pick it up in your size, and you are going to take it into the fitting room and try it on! Do not allow your head to interfere. No analysis of whether or not it is practical, no looking at the price tag – if it makes you feel excited inside, then grab it and go and express it on the outside!

Once you have it on, look at yourself in the mirror, how do you feel? Think of One adjective to describe your mood, for example, sexy, classy, fabulous, daring, bold, beautiful. Hold onto this word and do not let it go. Take off the outfit, and still, do not look at the price tag. Simply put it back where you got it from and leave the shop, without feeling deflated that it is out of your price range, but holding onto the buzz that you just felt as seeing yourself in something you truly like, but would not normally try on.

Before you head home, I now want you to treat yourself. I appreciate that we all have different budgets, so I have kept this little list in the low end of pricing. Ideally, if you can, you will treat yourself to all three items. But if this really is not possible, just get one. The items do not have to be the best that you can buy, a cheap alternative is great, as you are only going to use the item/s for the next two weeks. They are as follows:

a red lipstick, or if this shade is just not right for your skin tone, a tinted gloss that you can add to your everyday colour to spice things up. Do not stick to the safe, plain option. I want you to feel the rush of pushing your boundaries

A pair of stockings or hold ups. Choose the look and texture that will make you *feel* sexy and sensual.

A simple garter

When this little trip is over, why not head to the nearest coffee bar and treat yourself to a drink?

Back at home, take the photo that you took of yourself in the fabulous outfit, and attach it to your Vision board. Take a marker pen, or something similar, and write the adjective that you chose to describe how you felt on the photo somewhere.

Now let's move onto the second task for this weekend, this is something that you can do from home and shouldn't take more than five minutes. The majority of it, is reading this following information. Find your favourite pair of heels, put them on and spend the rest of the weekend wearing them, Whether it be around the house, to the supermarket, or just sitting watching TV. Get used to feeling fantastic and feminine and don't save such things for 'special occasions' only. ***Every day of your life should be a celebration.***

Heels accentuate your physical female form, and it is said that the arching of your bottom makes like a mating signal to the male species. Now this is not so much about attracting a male, and I appreciate that you may even be happily married, but I want *you* to *feel* feminine, sexual, and sensual.

'I want you to tap into the connection between the physical self and your Inner Goddess, and in the words of Shania Twain, be able to say 'man I feel like a woman!'.

Now let's look at the rest of week two. Here are your morning and evening routines.

A.M You will begin each day of this week (and next also) in the same way – by waking and drinking in your Goddess vision board. This will become a staple of this programme, and hopefully, at the end of the 21 days it will indeed have become a habit, that you will continue to use long term.

Once you have done so, depending on which order you prefer to do things, also stick to the cleansing ritual, hot water and lemon (or as an alternative, do try Green Tea) and the application of your Goddess potion. This will have you feeling fabulous in 15 minutes! Imagine that the potion is a layer between yourself and the Universal energy, It draws positive energy towards you and then converts it and transfers it, sending it inwards, to nourish your Inner Goddess.

Now – when you prepare yourself to 'face' the world, do you wear makeup? If not why not? If it is simply because you do not like it, then this is fine, It's personal choice. But if it's because you just can't be bothered to find the time, well all of that is about to change. I am not expecting you to work miracles and go from being Miss mascara to Miss Full face and a little bit more in one week. Like I said before, Unleashing your Inner Goddess does not have to involve being anything or anyone that you are not. The idea is, to enhance YOU. To experiment with one or two tools that will take you out of your comfort zone, and have one of two possible effects. Those being, that you will either like how it makes you feel, or you won't. Remember **'it is through sometimes experiencing what we don't want, that we work out what we do want'** and vice versa. So there really are no rights and wrongs in these tasks that I set you, as the outcome, in one way or another, really will guide you back towards your most authentic self.

As you get ready for the day ahead, whatever that day may involved, put on a coating of lipstick or the gloss that you bought. If you wear makeup anyway, great just slot this into your usual routine, but if you don't you may also like to add a little mascara to 'balance' your features out, as it may look too harsh with just your lips made up. How do you feel right after you have first applied it? Is your instinct to wipe it off? Or do you actually like what is looking back at you from the mirror? Make a mental note of this.

Next, as you dress, I want you to wear the stockings/hold ups that you bought at the weekend. You do not need to wear an outfit to match. This is the fun part. If you wear a skirt to work, then great, you can pop the stockings on and you won't look out of place. But ideally, I want you to try and wear trousers if possible. I like to carry out this exercise wearing jeans! Pop the stockings on underneath, and then ideally, match them with heels. How do you feel, knowing that you have such seductive attire on under something, and no one else has a clue? It's like your secret weapon. Instantly, with your heels on, your lips, and your stockings, you will feel seductive, feminine and you will stand taller. People may notice that something is different about you, but may not be able to put their finger on it. Enjoy any compliments, and make notes on how this experience goes all week.

Carry this routine out every day of week two.

P.M In the evenings this week, you can still slot in bathing rituals, using oils that you desire, to suit your mood. I want you to find time, make time, every evening so that you have at least 30 minutes to yourself. I know that this may feel impossible, especially if you have children. But each and every one of us deserves a little alone/me time on a daily basis. You can use this time in any way that you so wish, but on the promise, that it is something 'pleasurable' to you. No chores, no obligatory, norm. Think along the lines of a nice treat with a glass of wine, or a bar of chocolate, a hot chocolate, meditation, a massage, candles and oils, a face mask, manicure. Nothing extravagant, but pamper yourself, and nourish your soul for 30 mins to an hour, every evening. Time alone is important, as it helps you reconnect with your soul, your Inner Goddess, and it also gives you time to refer to this book, or spend some 'time out' just thinking, relaxing. There is a lot that you may want to reflect on. So many of us have a hard time justifying making time purely for ourselves, we are programmed to be wife, girlfriend, mother, daughter, sister, friend, but before all of that, should come being 'YOU'.

Only when have recharged your own batteries, and are fully connected to your personal energy source, your

Inner Goddess, can you start to think about giving energy back out to others'

At bed time, or just before bed, light a candle. Ideally, a red one, and spend five minutes alone, if possible, in front of the mirror. I want you to think of five things about yourself that you like. Do not allow any negative thoughts to come into play. If and when they do, almost 'zap' them away, just stop them right in their tracks, and replace them with the positive. Make a note here of the five things that you came up with:

1

2

3

4

5

Focusing on these things, get yourself ready for bed, taking time to prepare yourself for your meditation/visualisation technique that I am about to teach you. Maybe you prefer to have a bath in the evening, if so, try adding some candlelight and essential oils, and treat yourself again to a cleansing experience, and apply your Goddess potion allover your body. If you don't bathe, remember to remove your make-up with your cleanser, but don't just rub it off, think again, of yourself as a porcelain, hand-painted doll, and take great care and respect over it. Imagine that you are wiping away all of the day's energy, especially the negative, and then treat yourself to a facial massage.

Facial Massage is wonderful for relaxation after a long day, but can also prevent ageing, help to remove toxins, and get the lymph system working. Take a little moisturiser and simply massage your face gently, focusing on your brow and forehead. Feel the tension and stress leaving your body, and when you are in a relaxed state, you may like to try out the following exercise. If you can do it at bedtime, with your Vision board handy, even better, *but it's up to you.*

If you are lay down in bed, then spend a simple ten minutes drinking in your vision board, and then as you begin to feel sleepy, close your eyes and imagine that you are on a sandy beach. Feel the warmth of the sun on your skin, and the sand between your toes. Listen for the sound of the ocean, and the birds in the sky. The beach is secluded, only *you* walk alone on it, in the distance are some large rocks, where you can see the water, lapping against the side of them. Keep walking towards these rocks, and count your footsteps as you go. One, two, three, four, five, six, seven, eight… Focus on your toes, one foot in front of the other, effortlessly. When you arrive at the rocks, you pull yourself up onto the surface of the one closest to you, and you lie down, spread out, ready to absorb the sun's rays.

The sun is extremely powerful today, and a week ago, you would have felt overpowered by it. But this week, you are open to it, and invite it in, to penetrate your soul. The rays are drawn to you, as if you are a piece of absorbent material. They swirl and swoop, down to you, you are their target, and you are receptive to their arrival. They bathe you, you are coated in bright sunlight, and as you feel the warmth and pleasure from this, you begin to notice the rays take on a life of their own, and direct themselves towards the top of your head.

They find an entrance in, and begin to trickle down into your head, passing down through your face, into your neck, flooding through your shoulders and heart chakra, filling your arms – once the energy reaches your finger tips, you can feel them tingle, and you are almost electric, a current is building up inside of you, ready to be passed on to others. Some of them do an about turn, and pass back through your heart chakra, down into your abdomen, soothing any knots of tension that may have gathered here, and filling your hip and pelvic area. This is the area that represents your femininity. Allow the energy to take on strength here, as your sexual energy mixes with it and it is exemplified. It passes down, into your nether regions, and down into your thighs, until it works its way down to the tips of your toes.

Like an electrically charged instrument, you are a buzz of energy, and your sexuality, your sensuality has been mingled with this Universal energy and is going to remain within you as you sleep, until when you wake.

The following day, as you wake to see your Goddess Vision Board, you will feel aroused by the thought of this sexually charged you, stepping out of bed, and preparing herself to take her Goddess energy out into the real world. You are unstoppable and untouchable, and no matter what happens during your day, nothing can hold you back. You are so vibrantly energised, that anything that does not match this rolls off you like water off a duck's back.

Now, as a charged, and daring Vixen, in tune with her Inner energy/Inner Goddess, let's move into week three.

WEEK THREE

Welcome to week three of the Unleash Your Inner Goddess Programme!

MISSION: To look at how to maintain your connection with your Inner Goddess and re-charge your personal energy, any time, any place.

This week we will look at the following: How to maintain the connection between the Vixen and Inner Goddess, and how to recharge the Goddess through tuning into the Universal energy.

Tools and techniques include: Vision board, Goddess cleansing ritual, Visualisations, Dinner Date Exercise

Weekend: Vixen and Inner Goddess go on a date

Weekdays: A.M and P.M routines

You will need the following:
- *Goddess Cleansing Lotion*
- *Goddess Potion*
- *Vision Board*
- *Stockings, garter, makeup as outlined in week two*
- *A pink candle*
- *A piece of rose quartz*

This week, you are going to be feeling more confident than you have in a long time. And if you are still working on that side to things, you will certainly be feeling more 'self aware'. A large majority of the reason as to why we can remain closed off to our Inner Goddess, is simply because we are so busy running ourselves ragged, and focusing on everything and everyone else that we lose sight of ourselves. But by now, we have established, that you cannot begin to think about giving pure, genuine love and energy out to those around you, until you have conjured it up within yourself first. If you do not take care of yourself primarily, you will be exhausted, and running on empty, and in time, will start to resent having to be there for others. I look at energy and your relationship with others, in particular romance, in section three of this book.

Back to this week though, and our main mission is to take the newly charged you out into the outside world, and look at how you can now communicate with others whilst remaining in tune with your Inner Goddess. I want us to practise body language, stress control, and general self presentation skills.

LOVE BLOSSOMS – VIXEN AND INNER GODDESS

Now that you are into week three, you will be feeling much more in tune with your Inner Goddess on a daily basis, and keeping the Victim at bay should be something that you enjoy to do. To enhance the more exclusive relationship that has formed between the Vixen and the Inner Goddess, I am going to take you out of your comfort zone a little, and put your Inner Goddess to the test. Let's see if this couple really can go out in public without the interference from that unwanted third party – The Victim.

This weekend your task is to take yourself out to dinner. Yes, you read that correctly, and I know that this may seem totally over whelming for many of you. But as someone who travelled the world *alone* (and right after a break up when I was feeling particularly low and vulnerable), trust me when I tell you, that once you have done something like this, you feel amazing!

So here is the lowdown:

Vixen and Inner Goddess go on a date.

Now think about it just in just those terms. That you, as Vixen, are taking your Inner Goddess out on a dinner date. Remember back to section one, where you met your Inner Goddess? You imagined her as a character in her own right and thought about all of her attributes in comparison to her arch enemy, the Victim. When you go out to eat, you are not totally alone, as you are taking your Goddess with you, and if at any time you feel uncomfortable, you can turn to her for advice and support.

Think about where you would like to go, and what time of day you are most comfortable with doing this. Maybe choose a lunchtime menu, so that you appear like a lady who lunches amidst a busy day shopping. Plenty of people do this, and maybe you already do yourself, so this won't be a mission for you, but a pleasure.

Holding onto that word… *pleasure* – think of this experience as just that. There are so few moments that we get to spend entirely with ourselves, and this is one of them. So relish the alone time, and find comfort in your Inner thoughts. You do not need to sit in a central location, or attract masses of attention to yourself. If it is a nice day, you may even like to choose a quiet, outdoor table where you can sit and watch the world pass by.

Now, as this is a 'date', you are to spend time before leaving the house, preparing yourself accordingly. Present yourself to YOU in just the same way that you would present yourself to anyone else. Ideally, wear your stockings under your outfit as described in week two, and take care with a little make up, perfume, and heels if you feel comfortable.

As you head out on your date, imagine that you have a golden ball of energy that is radiating in your pelvic area. Feel your feminine energy expand and contract, and allow yourself to be guided from this region. Think of this energy as being magnetic to the Universal energy, and the two are constantly engaged.

Thus, your Inner energy, your Inner Goddess, is connected to to your external surroundings, and you are guided forwards on your journey with ease and elegance, almost gliding along, drawn to the energy that calls you ahead. Focusing on this exchange of energy, you will remain engaged in the present moment, and this will keep chitter chatter, fear and the Victim at bay. If you do find yourself distracted from your focus, then simply turn your thoughts back inwards. If your ball of energy seems to be lacking in strength, and you are having difficulty locating it, then turn your attention to the sun's rays. Even if the sun is not visible, it is always there, an ever present source of immeasurable power. So allow it to recharge your energy, and then focus on the interchange and reconnection between the two sources, the internal and external.

No matter what is going on around you, the people outside the restaurant or cafe bar, the distractions in the distance, the sound of sirens or passing buses – just remain in contact with and focused on your current connection from your pelvis to the Universe. You are a Goddess in all her glory, moving in time with the Universal rhythm.

Throughout the entire dining experience, remain connected to this ball of energy and as you sit alone, focus on it radiating inwards as well as outwards. Not only is it connected to the external energy, it is also connected to your internal energy, It is an energy made up from one – it comes from the Universe, but so do you, and your Inner Goddess is connected to the Universe, and vice versa. Feel your affinity with this expansive, never ending life source, and acknowledge your place in the grander scheme of things.

Maintaining our personal energy, staying connected to our Inner Goddess, does not just benefit our self, it works on a much wider scale. It has an impact on those directly close to you, friends, family, lovers – those who you share yourself and your time and energy with. Those who you *give* your energy to. Then, it has an effect upon the energy of the Universe as a whole. If we all work to maintain a positive and upbeat energy output, then we could really make a difference to the future of the planet. As Ghandi once said, **'Be the change that you wish to see in the world'** I will look at this connection in greater detail in section three of the book.

But as you sit over lunch, try and zone into your inner calm. That private oasis, where you become aware only of your inner energy connected to the Universal energy, and notice how this feels. When you can reach this place of contentment, you are well on your way to knowing how to find inner peace in almost any situation from now on. You can implement this technique, not only to ground yourself, but to bring yourself into harmony with the 'bigger picture', and flow in affinity with the Universal energy, which is where you will discover a magical 'shift'. You will begin to move through your moments, as just that – little moments. Focusing in just that moment, (remember in and not on), you will find that Chitter chatter and fear will become less and less frequent in your day to day experience. As you utilise your tools and techniques that keep you grounded in the moment, connected to your Inner Goddess, you become aware that with every passing moment and thought, you have the power to create your destiny.

Hopefully, this lunch is an enjoyable and unique experience, and despite being surrounded by lots of strangers, you were able to feel comfortable within your own skin, safe within your own zone/bubble and able to detach from paranoia and worry, about what everybody else around was thinking of you. Trust me, in general people are so wrapped up in their own worries that they don't have time to focus so much on you.

For the rest of this weekend, I want you to simply relax, and keep practising this technique, of zoning into your personal energy and space. You can do it anywhere you like!
Now let's move onto your morning and evening exercises for week three:

A.M As in week one and two, you will be waking up to your Goddess Vision Board. This should definitely by now, be feeling completely natural to you. Allow yourself to drink it in for ten minutes before rising. After hot water and lemon, and your cleansing routine or a cleansing bath/shower, you will repeat the steps as outlined in week two morning routine, in taking a little care with your make-up and putting on your secret weapons, the stockings, garter and heels, under whatever it is that you are wearing for the day, even if you are staying in the house in your pyjamas!

Next, I want you to practise the exercise that you did on your date with your Inner Goddess, and focus on your ball of energy that is building for the day ahead. Visualise it and connect with it *before* you leave the house. You should still do this if you don't plan to leave the house too. Feel it moving around, from your heart chakra, to your pelvic region. Connect to your feminine energy, tune into your Inner Goddess. Next, move onto noticing how this energy is connected to the Universal energy, and feel the giving and receiving taking place in equal balance. As you head get through your day, always remain in contact with this connection and as you glide through your day, notice when you feel yourself slipping. Do not let chitter chatter and worry and fear creep in, keep your energy and resistance to negative energies high.

If and when you come into contact with others, notice how they react to you. How are you presenting yourself? Stand tall, allow the energy to move freely from the top of your head right down to the tips of your toes. Feel it gather in the tips of your fingers, until it almost feels like you are electro magnetic. Know, that you have the power to pass this energy on to others and make a positive difference to their energy field, and their day. Think of this like a 'pass it on, pay it forward' exercise. If you can positively influence just one person today, then that person will pass it on to someone that they come into contact and so on, and this will have a knock on effect on a much larger scale.

'Attitudes are contagious – is yours worth catching?'

It can be slightly overwhelming, I know, to understand just how much influence your thoughts and attitude has over not only choosing your character, creating your own destiny, but now I am also throwing into your personal responsibility to others, and the planet! But it does not have to be complicated, that's the beauty of it! You are actually learning how to simplify your life and find inner peace and happiness, and as a result, at least influence your immediate personal space in the process.

P.M For your evening routine in week three, I want you to try and move away from doing any exercises that are still looking at keeping the Victim at bay. By now, I hope that you are feeling completely in touch with your Inner Goddess, and I want to look at how to strengthen this feeling.

Do make time to relax and have some 'you' time, and if you feel like you need a pick me up, there are always the bathing and cleansing rituals to try out, but try and focus on welcoming your Inner Goddess into your every day life, if you can, focus on her and look forwards now, rather than look back and work on cleansing away the Victim. This only really needs to be done on those days when you really are totally lost, or in periods where something bad has happened in your life and you are struggling on a daily basis to cope. But on normal days, remember that it's okay to have moments where you don't feel on top form, and have a little fear or worry. To some extent, these emotions are actually a part of every day life, we are not looking to eradicate them altogether, as then we would be totally unbalanced. We just want to negate any unnecessary worrying that has been holding you back.

Now, every evening this week, I want you to connect with the moon. Just as the sun holds a Universal energy, so does the moon. But the moons energy is specifically in contact with our feminine energies, and our Inner Goddess. As I have explained throughout the book, the moon affects the tides, our emotions, fertility, our menstrual cycle. La Luna as I like to call her, is extremely powerful and in witchcraft, spells are cast according to the energies of the moon. She is a Goddess in her own right, possibly the most powerful one of the entire Universe. It is good to check out the moon cycle via the Internet, and know when you are approaching a full moon, new moon, when it is waning and when it is waxing. Once you become aware of where we are at with the moon's cycle, you can monitor your moods, and work out whether they are based upon an emotion that needs to be looked at, hormones, or the influence of the moon.

Late in the evening, before bed, light a pink candle and take a piece of rose quartz. You can get both via the Internet, or from any new age/spiritual shop. Try out the exercise below:

Inner Goddess talks to Luna Goddess

Our great symbol for the Goddess is the moon, whose three aspects reflect the three stages in women's lives and whose cycles of waxing and waning coincide with women's menstrual cycles. – Carol P. Christ

Obviously, finding out the position of the moon in her cycle as you read this book, is something that only you can do. I cannot predict where it will be, because I don't know when you will be reading this! So I am going to suggest that you work out where the moon is (is it waning, waxing, new, full), and then make a note of it on your calender. Then, try and communicate with the moon daily from here on, so that you really get in tune with her. The position of the moon can alter how you communicate with your Inner Goddess, because she has a real influence on how we may be feeling from one week to the next. To know whether this is linked to the moon helps us work out how to deal with it, as I explained above.

Also, you can combine your Inner Goddess, and your own energy and power, with that of the Lunar cycle, in order to use this joint energy to make changes to your life.

I have discussed how the Universal energy can work with yours, in order to create the life that you desire (law of attraction). Well, you can work the Lunar Calender into this equation also. For example, when wanting to focus on growth, change, and creation of a new period in your life, then visualising those things happening at bed time, under the new moon of the moon will add strength to your visualisations and the manifestation of what you are looking to create. If you are hoping to attract love and romance into your life, and you want to work on self love and confidence, then the full moon is wonderful for these kind of desires.

So, whilst in bed, having looked at your Goddess Vision board and 'drank' that in for at least 10-15 minutes, you can close your eyes, and follow this simple visualisation technique:

Imagine the moon is full and it is in the sky above you. You are lay down on the grass in the middle of a large field. You cannot see the parameters of this field, the further you look out, the more you see darkness. Right above you, is a powerful, radiant cool Moon. It works in the same way as the sun, sending its rays down to you, as you absorb them into your body. Only the moon recharges not only your general energy, but your Goddess energy, your female energy. We are all made up of masculine and feminine energy, think of the yin and yang. We need a balance between the two in order to achieve harmony. But a woman possesses a dominance in feminine energy that enables her to nurture, to be a mother, to be a care giver, to reproduce, and to attract a male in order to do so. So allow the moon to penetrate deep into your soul, and feed and nourish your Inner

Goddess. Feel the coolness of her rays, very different to the warmth of the sun. Feel this energy gather in your heart chakra, your pelvic region. If you have any female problems such as PMS, hormonal imbalances, fertility issues, then invite the moon in to help things run on more even keel. Feel her bathe your skin, soothe away any tension, or issues that you may have about your appearance. Visualise yourself feeling and looking at your optimum best.

From this week onwards, try and communicate with the moon as often as possible. She will preserve the inner peace that you have found over these 21 days, and through reading the wisdom within this book. Allow her to preserve the energy, and for the sun to recharge it when you feel yourself lacking. Think of the moon as being able to seal any energy that you have generated during the day time. She takes the energy, mixes it with her own, and with your personal Inner Goddess energy and adds the feminine touch to the mix.

NOW THAT THE 21 DAYS ARE UP...

Over the course of the three week programme, you will have naturally become more aware of your Inner Goddess' daily presence. The exercises that you followed, moved you from simply thinking about how you relate to her, to actually doing it. You are not only aware of her existence, you now know how to nurture her, care for her, re-charge her and preserve her. Hopefully, with gliding through the 21 days, you have naturally shed the associations of the Victim, and are better equipped to not only recognise when you are listening to Fear, but to also implement tools that will zap it away, and allow your Inner Goddess to take over.

Now that this internal shift has taken place, you find that with each day that passes, you are feeling more and more like the Vixen that you were born to be. Totally in tune with your Inner Goddess, and beginning to create the life that you desire.

The idea of the 21 day programme is not to completely magically transform you within such a short space of time. Do not expect to feel like a whole other person, and be disappointed when you do not. The idea of this book is to help you to reconnect with your Inner Goddess, and Unleash her to the world. Your Inner Goddess, is quite simply, your most authentic self. She is YOU. She is not the embodiment of perfection, because perfection does not exist. She is the beauty and contrast of you on good and bad days. She is not happy *all* of the time. This would be unrealistic and false. But she knows how to implement tools to help her cope with the tough times. She is self aware and patient. She knows how to work out how she is feeling and then act rather than react accordingly. Focusing 'in' the present moment, you are able to create your immediate happiness, and also longer term desires and goals. You are now aware of your place in the Universe and the beauty that is Universal energy. You can tune into this energy when you need to recharge your own batteries, and you also know that when you remain connected to this energy and stay focused in the moment and just 'feel', you can create the future that you desire. All in all, you have the ability to remain constant, protected in a bubble of energy, taking the mantra *'you cannot alter the direction of the wind, but you can always adjust your sails'* wherever you go.

If and when life does throw disaster your way, you are much better equipped to 'handle it'. You know that everything can be used as a lesson, and that baggage is of no use for your future. It simply weighs you down. You see, you no longer choose to be a Victim of life and for things to be beyond your control – and you know that the more you can remain positively charged, the greater presence you are around those that you love. Energy is contagious, so guilt, and being a martyr, is no longer necessary. You have a higher purpose, and in choosing this very book, you were being drawn to your acknowledgement of the this, and the life path that you are destined to take.

You were never put on this earth simply to settle for a half hearted ride, you are here for a reason, and you have more potential and influence on things than you ever realised.

But now that you have this sacred knowledge – how will you utilise it? Will you pass it on? If you can think of just one other person on this planet who may benefit from this programme then imagine the change that you could make to their life, by guiding them! The friend who is so often downtrodden, the one who plays Victim to men, the girl who over apologizes for everything. We spend so much of our time analysing things in life, that we miss the magic of the moment. A classic example, is the obscene amount of time, that we sit around trying to second guess what the man in our life wants. Constantly trying to be what we think he wants us to be – (or she of course!) Second guessing our every move so that we do not 'rock the boat'. In Section three, I look in more detail at this kind of scenario, but I hope that already, you are starting to work out, that all of these actions, are simply a waste of time and energy! Life could be and should be so much simpler than a lot of us make it.

Staying true to our most authentic self, and then interacting with others from this place of inner security improves relationships of all kinds and on all levels.

We are entering a new age, where more and more people are becoming 'spiritually enlightened'. There has been the recognition, that if we all come together in unity, then a higher state of existence, love and peace really will take over. And the things that I am passing onto you, your Inner power, the Universal energy, has been around since the dawn of time.

section three

21 days and beyond...

the little guide to standing tall

21 DAYS AND BEYOND...
THE LITTLE GUIDE TO STANDING TALL

This part of the book is something that I hope that you can refer to over and over again. My intention in this section, is to offer you words of wisdom, and a reminder of your inner strength at times when you may need it most.

It's one thing to decide to rediscover yourself, another to follow the 21 day programme, but the real challenge comes from life *after* you have put this book down.

'It is when the initial buzz of Unleashing your Inner Goddess wears off – and life throws you yet another curve ball – that the real need for this book kicks in.'

To maintain the simplicity, that I hope that you have now discovered in your life, takes a daily concerted effort. Sure, the idea is that your mind will feel much clearer, you glide through life almost effortlessly, but this lifestyle change is a choice that you have to choose to follow every day for the rest of your life. Sounds difficult right? Well it's not, not really. I am going to share with you, in my own words and from my own experience, how I end and start my day, the methods that I use in order to keep my mind and spirit on track. Please bear with me, as I am going to speak from my subconscious here, I want the words to come from my heart, I will let my Inner Goddess speak directly to you, and with you. It may not make a great deal of sense but it is for you to take what you will or will not from my personal experience.

When I wake every morning, the first thing that I do, is purse my lips together. Strange huh? Well yes, yes it is! But this little physical action has somehow become an anchor for my subconscious. To To anchor something involves the attachment of a physical gesture with an emotion, thought or feeling. In the future, any time that you then carry out this gesture (or have it done to you, e.g a touch on the arm by another), the subconscious mind will trigger off the associated emotion, thought or feeling. In order to attach this gesture with a particular mindset, in this case, the mindset of peace and tranquility, I practised meditation for a short period. During meditation, I focused on (visualised) a hilltop. And on this hilltop, I discovered complete and utter relaxation. The hilltop was covered in soft, spongy grass, that felt warm on the bare soles of my feet. Warm from the pool of glowing sunlight that oozed from the sky above and enveloped me with love and care. I simply stood and basked in this sunlight, allowing it to circle around me, and penetrate every pore, until I was electrically charged with this immense Universal power.

To the left of me was the hilltop edge, a sheer drop-that exited down to the most wonderfully golden sandy beach. The Ocean was radiant, and if I attempted to look out, I had to cover my eyes with my hand, for the reflection of the sunlight, bouncing off the gentle ripples of the crystal clear water nearly blinded me. All around me, was peace and quiet. I could only hear the odd gull in the distance, circling the water, seeking lunch. The breeze was my main focus, it carried the sun's rays with it, and my energy strengthened, like an appliance on charge. I was close to full power. Feeling myself totally connected to the Universal energy via the sun's connection, I realised that the sun and moon are two of the most powerful natural sources of life energy.

I realised, that whenever I felt tired, withdrawn or simply disconnected from my source energy (the Universal energy that feeds me, and my Inner Goddess) ,instead of focusing on that feeling (what you focus on grows, remember..) I could instantly transport myself back to this place of security. My very own safe haven. Within minutes, I could connect myself to the sun, or if it were night time, the moon and I would find my mind completely cleared of its whirring thoughts and my body in a state of instant soothing and relaxation.

The pursing of the lips just happened to be something that I naturally did/do as soon as I began to feel the effects of the solar or lunar recharging/awakening.

If for example, I am out, maybe at work, or on a train, and I cannot close my eyes and meditate like I do when I am in bed in the morning or evening, I simply purse my lips and daydream my way back to my secret place.

And relax….

The above technique that I have shared with you, is something that I welcome you to try for yourself. I find it a wonderful little exercise, but also, a powerful reminder. It reminds me of my presence and place in this cosmic Universe. It connects me to the sun, the moon, to everything and everyone. We are all a part of this Source energy. We truly are all one.

Carrying out this simple but effective exercise, not only keeps me grounded in the moment, it also maintains my connection to the external source, the law of attraction. I am able to feel energy flowing within me and without me. There is the ever present flow of giving and receiving energy, love, joy and gratitude. It embodies all that this book and its philosophy intends to be.

'Connect your Inner Goddess with the Source energy from the Universe via the sun or moon, and feel your chakras open! Spark a connection, a link from deep within yourself, to way beyond and outside of yourself and notice the flow of the giving and receiving of love and energy.'

So there we have it! I do this little ritual every night before I go to sleep, visualising myself connecting to the moons energy, and every morning before I get up, connecting myself to the suns energy. Not only is it a way to energise myself and also snap myself back into the present moment in terms of its immediate effects to mind and body, it also serves as a reminder of the bigger picture.

But what about those moments during the day, when I find myself becoming disconnected from my Inner Goddess?

Well, a little addition to the above routine, was the incorporation of a 'crystal'. I favoured a nice cold chunk of pink rose quartz. You can of course choose something that you feel most applicable to your individual personality and requirements. Requirements? – Yes.. crystals are renowned the world over, for their 'healing' properties and can do all manner of things for mind, body and spirit.

I have chosen a short but sweet selection of 'Inner Goddess' crystals to give you a start, but the best thing to do, is pop along to a shop that sells them and have a read and a feel. You will know from the sensation of holding one in your hand, whether or not it works with your energy.

The idea of the crystal, is that you introduce it into your twice daily meditation/connection to source exercise, and simply hold it in your hand throughout the process. The crystal will mix with your aura, your energy, and will soothe you (or energise you!) with its personal properties, as well as absorb *your* energy and become charged with your peaceful state. Then, during the day, when you feel yourself slipping out of sync with your Inner Goddess, you can take the crystal from your pocket, and connect with it in an instant. Again, it will serve like an anchor, to jerk your subconscious mind into remembering your daily mission.

Inner Goddess Crystals

Rose Quartz: Love and calm. Rose quartz is one of the most popular crystals along with amethyst and clear quartz. It has a calming and soothing energy. It promotes self-love and helps overcome feelings of not being 'good' enough, self-criticism and resentment. It reminds us that when you love yourself and are happy in the moment there is no need for haste. Rose quartz embraces the one true currency of life, love.

Clear Quartz: One of the most powerful all rounders, great for general healing and purifying, helps you to connect your Inner self. Clear quartz helps to dispel negative energy you may have absorbed from other people. If you tend to put yourself down, quartz may help you fight that feeling. It is good to hold or have around whenever you feel foggy, uncertain or would like to see your way more clearly. It is one of the most frequently used crystals because of its wide-ranging benefits.

Citrine: the sunshine stone, also known as the 'cuddle stone' is like a big comforting hug! Citrine is a stone that often reflects light in a sunny and warming fashion. It is a crystal of creativity and positive expression of who we truly are. This gives us a good feeling and impacts on those around us in a positive way.

Amethyst: reminds us of the spiritual thread that runs through our life and can be used as a tool to aid spiritual awakening and intuition. Amethyst can bring a calming influence and therefore be of great help in times of change. It's excellent to hold or have by you when you're practising meditation and when placed in a room it can help absorb negativity. Placed under the pillow it may help you sleep better.

THE LITTLE GUIDE TO STANDING TALL

This is where I will relate all that we have covered, to a variety of possible everyday situations that you may find yourself in. Like a friend and coach on the bookshelf, I can be turned to for advice at any given time further down the line. I will compare and contrast, looking at how the Victim, Vixen and Inner Goddess would handle themselves in each scenario.

The topics that I will cover are as follows:
- *Love thyself*
- *Love*
- *Fear and Love*
- *Create your Ideal Partner*
- *Dating*
- *Kicking the ass of Jealousy and Fear*
- *Inner Goddess tackles a broken heart, inc the 'Feel and Heal' technique*
- *You can't please everyone – put yourself first*

Love thyself....

Loving crack of the whip #15: *If you do not love yourself, how you can you expect anybody else to love you? It's so very simple. Until you are operating from your most authentic self and are in tune with your Inner Goddess, the 'you' that you present to others, is simply a half hearted version of the real you. You are*

> *allowing them to fall in love with a false representation of who*
> *you are and what you stand for. Give yourself a chance – stop*
> *being your own worst enemy.*

I don't really need to say too much here. If and when you are doubting yourself, or having an off day – think back to the main theme of this book as a whole.

'You cannot alter the direction of the wind, but you can always adjust your sails'. Life is a cycle of ups and downs. We cannot control what life (and others around us) throws at us but we *can* adjust and control how we let things affect us. We have the choice between *acting* and *reacting*. We can take absolutely any scenario that we may find ourselves in and use it as an opportunity to expand and grow. Life is one big challenge and just because bad things may come our way, does not mean that we have to *choose* to play the *role* of the Victim. However, being a Vixen, in tune with her Inner Goddess, does not mean that I am suggesting that you suddenly stop feeling, and become some sort of super hero, like wonder woman. I am not suggesting that you become a more fine tuned, perfect version of your former self because *perfection does not exist*. Unleashing your Inner Goddess, and being your most authentic self means being comfortable with yourself, warts and all. Embracing your past, taking it peacefully with you into your present, and choosing to use your mind power to focus forwards rather than backwards. Once you can do this, you can begin to connect your inner energy (your Goddess) to that of the Universe, and work with the law of attraction, in order to manifest the life that you truly desire and deserve. The time is now – don't even waste another moment looking backwards, as Ghandi once said 'be the change that you want to see in the world'. Be pro-active and if you are not content with who you are where you are, then make a difference. YOU are in control of you.

If and when you are questioning yourself, or your role in the world, then read the above summary as often as possible to remind yourself of the task in hand.

You are the creator of your own destiny, and you have the power to be exactly *where* you want to be, be exactly *who* you want to be.

Jot down the opening quote of this book and carry it around with you:

There is no passion to be found playing small – in settling for a life that is less than the one you are capable of living. – Nelson Mandela

I will leave this section at that because I don't want to repeat all that we have already covered.

Love....

> **Loving crack of the whip #16:** *What is it that you fear? Denying our Inner Goddess means that we deny the chance to find a real, balanced and honest love. If you come together with another, operating at a fraction of your potential then you do not come together as two wholes. The relationship will be unbalanced from the beginning. Learning to love yourself is the quickest route to finding your true love in another.*

Moving onto love – as let's face it, a lot of us are particularly interested in this area and how to date successfully, maintain a relationship and just generally troubleshoot when it comes to relating to the opposite sex. However, I don't necessarily want to refer to love as being associated with 'men'. I celebrate sexuality in all its variants, and believe that the majority of us, if not all of us, have the capability to be attracted to both the opposite, and also the same sex.

The key thing to take from this section on love, is that when you refuse to adopt the role of the Victim, and operate from a place of being a Vixen, in touch with her Inner Goddess, then relationships of all kinds will improve.

'As soon as you begin to live each day of your life, as your most authentic self, you will be in perfect alignment to attract those people most suited and destined to accompany you on your life path'.

Be prepared, that when you begin to ooze confidence, and speak from your heart and soul, those in your life who are not best suited to the real you may accuse you of having changed, and 'friends' and lovers may even leave your life. But the pros of unleashing your Inner Goddess far outweigh the cons. Why would you want to live your life operating from a place that is out of touch with your soul, out of alignment with source energy? Not to mention that the majority of relationship issues arise, because there is discord, disharmony, due to one or more parties feeling unfulfilled, misunderstood and disconnected.

But when we are connected to our Inner Goddess, we instantly feel an inner happiness that far outweighs anything that we can experience coming via another.

There is a saying, that when we fall in love with another, we are actually also falling in love with ourselves. Isn't it sad, that all too often, it takes us meeting another equally wonderful human being, to Unleash our most authentic self, and feel inner peace and happiness? Why is it not possible to reach this state of bliss solo? Well, that's my point exactly – it *is* possible! Often, when we feel dissatisfied within our romantic relationship, (or any other – love is applicable to all kinds of interactions) we look directly to our partner for an explanation as to why.

We question 'is it this, or that? What is it/why is it that I feel this feeling?' We assume that there must be something in the relationship, or the other person, that is somehow to blame. We place all this emphasis on looking *externally*, when the true key to daily happiness lies *internally*. Making the internal shift to self sufficient happiness, takes the emphasis and pressure off our partner, and gives space for free flowing communication. So many issues within a relationship are fuelled by, you guessed it, our old friend 'Fear'. Let's look at that in more depth for a moment.

Fear and Love!

> **Loving crack of the whip #17**: *Allowing fear to hold you back in love, is causing you just as much frustration and pain as the heartache that you avoid will. So why not just take a gamble, and allow yourself to be happy? Is it really the idea of loss that you fear, or have we simply forgotten how to be happy?*

'Fear can stop you loving, love can stop your fear... fear can stop you loving, but it's not always that clear' (Love and Fear, Morcheeba).

I want you to make a list of all of the ways that you think fear can interfere with a relationship. This can be based upon your personal experience, or you can just write a general list.

Fear can operate in the following ways:

It stops people from approaching someone that they are attracted to

It makes people 'put on an act' , often feeling scared to then be themselves, in-case their love interest/new partner 'goes off them'

It gives rise to Jealousy – as people fear losing their partner to another, through fear of not being good enough

General fear of loss – loving and having your heartbroken. This can actually stop some people from even trying to find love!

Now, thinking back to how Fear often works alongside our role of the Victim – how can this tie into the area of love and relationships?

Well, simply put, when we allow fear to interfere, all manner of problems may arise, simply because the natural flow of giving and receiving love has been interrupted. As soon as Fear takes hold of you, you stop functioning at your optimum level. This has an immediate effect on YOU, because you will feel disconnected from your Inner Goddess, and Source energy. You may begin to have sleepless nights, feel stressed and snappy, and become distracted from other areas of your life. How can you maintain what resembles a healthy and balanced relationship with another, when you are not healthy and balanced within yourself?

How many times have you looked back upon your behaviour with a partner and felt annoyed at yourself, because you weren't acting like the real you? How many times have you broken up with someone you love and after time has passed, you have realised that your actions were that of a crazy person? There is nothing worse than acting through fear. It makes monsters of us in love and it can push people to make decisions that they may then later regret.

Don't allow Fear to push you back into playing the Victim and lose control of yourself and your relationship.

I know it is hard, because where love and matters of the heart are concerned, logicality goes out the window. But, do yourself justice. If things are going to go wrong, isn't it better to walk away knowing that at all times, you were true to yourself. You were a Vixen in tune with her Inner Goddess and therefore, if things did not match up to your energy, then maybe they just were not meant to be? Don't leave yourself with a ton of regret, looking back wishing 'if only I had done this or that'.

Also, going back to how we match up to our ideal partner when we are set to our optimum frequency (energy), and can only expect to meet the match most suited to us when we are our most authentic self, well how will you ever know if you are with the right person for you if you are not being the best you that you can be? I honestly believe that a lot of relationships fail over time, because people start out as being 'what they think their partner wants them to be' but as time passes, they can't keep it up and then when one or the other slides back into being themselves, the other half of the equation figures that they have 'changed' and that something is wrong.

Stop being your own worst enemy and just try and sit back and throw caution to the wind, and just trust, that if you are being true to yourself, the one most suited will come into alignment with you and things will be a breeze. Of course, no relationship is perfect! Just like people – perfection in love does not and should not exist. But isn't it better to give it your best shot and then if things do go wrong, know that there actually wasn't any more that you could have done, than to act like a Victim (or part Victim), and then wish that you had one more chance to 'prove who you really are'. Whilst you are not being true to yourself, how can you really know that you are even with the right person and don't you owe it to yourself to discover all that is out there destined for YOU?

There really is no better way to approach the dating world, than to do it coming from a place of being connected to your Inner Goddess.

So, *let's take a wander into the dating world, and look at some of the dramas that we may encounter along the way.*

First up, has to be looking for Love! It's a minefield out there right now, and it is harder than it has ever been to meet Mr Right! (or Miss Right!). Let's explore the options of how we can go from wondering what to do about it, to scoring that first date!

There are many ways available through which we can set about looking for someone to share our spiritual /life journey with. But unfortunately, in today's world, where the possibilities are endless, this has almost worked against us singletons, because competition is fierce, and sadly, the Internet fuels the notion that 'the grass could be greener' so let's just take a peek over that fence. After all, looking can't hurt anyone right?

It's no wonder that so many of us today, are confused and find it hard to know where to start, who to date, who to trust and what we actually want anymore.

Think of it like a menu – only there must be at least ten things on that menu that you really gotta have there and then. How on earth do you narrow it down and choose? Well, the first thing that I advise clients to do, before embarking upon even looking for a partner, is to clearly *define* and then *visualise* just who it is that you desire to meet.

Let's set about doing that right now. No time like the present huh?

Create your ideal partner!
No, I am not talking about a morph like figure made out of Plasticine. Although that would be a useful tool to have in your visualisation kit! But seriously, in order to expect the Universe

to deliver the kind of person that you hope to meet, you need to be very clear in your mind's eye about just who it is that you are looking for.

Now – you cannot use the law of attraction upon one specific person as such, because that is going against that person's free will. But you *can* visualise your ideal partner, and then the Universe will respond accordingly. So, how exactly can you go about this? Well, why not start, with writing a list? Jot down all of the attributes that your dream partner would have, and be totally honest with yourself, as again, this is for nobody else to read, but you. If you want to throw in things like 'great abs, model looks, rich' then do so. No one is here to judge. You have to be truly honest with YOURSELF. Life is not a dress rehearsal and none of us are getting any younger, so decide clearly who and what you want to create into your life and get serious about it. Think about what this person looks like, smells like, talks like.What are their interests, passions, dreams, tastes? Where do you see yourself meeting? Get as much information down as possible, let your imagination run wild. Once you have done this, you can then turn your goals and ideas into a daily visualisation exercise. Now we have done plenty of visualising and connecting with your subconscious mind throughout this journey so I won't bore you with the ins and outs in too much detail but just incase you need a re-cap, here is a brief summary/suggestion.:

Visualise your Ideal partner: For 10-15 minutes, maybe when you are lay in the bath, or comfy in bed, close your eyes and visualise the partner that you have described on the list. Imagine them in 3D. Do not be a spectator looking on at the scene, be a part of the scene. Imagine that you are actually there and that this moment is happening in real time. You closed your eyes and you were magically transported to another place and time, this secret otherworldly place, meant just for the two of you. Use all of your senses: what does your partner look like today, what do they smell like, what do they sound like? What are you talking about? Or are you touching, kissing. This is your fantasy, your safe place, created within your mind, so you can do whatever comes naturally here. Lose yourself in the moment and if there is a message that you would like to pass on to your dream partner, then this is the time and space within which to communicate with them.

Tip: Imagine that your heart is bursting with love, passion, joy and excitement. Your Inner Goddess, your energy, is totally in tune with your partner, and you focus on the steady flow of love that passes back and forth between you. Now, imagine, that from your heart chakra, this energy morphs into a rainbow style source of energy. Picture the energy leave your body and connect to your partner's heart chakra. Visualise and *feel* the two of you being connected.

Once you are lost in this connection, notice how the Universal Source energy swirls around the two of you. Think back to the hilltop that I told you about, and how the Sun or Moon's energy connects to you and is absorbed via your every pore. As the two of you stand in union, the Universal energy is also 'charging' you, individually, and in turn, as a couple. You are taking energy from Source, internalising it, and then passing it back and forth, and together, you are whipping up this energy, so that it becomes an unstoppable, all powerful, forever giving love.

'As you visualise this scenario taking place, you will be truly feeling the sensation, and as you know, when you feel what you desire, as though it is already happening, you set the wheels of the law of attraction in motion and it snaps up your intention and as good as promises you their delivery.'

I want you to pause for a moment now, maybe make yourself a cup of tea or coffee, and then get cosy, whilst I tell you a true story.

The train man is what he shall be forever known, because I visualised, and met the man of my dreams, but let him slip away. I did the exercise exactly as described above, and I imagined myself meeting my man in all manner of situation, but the main place that we seemed to connect, was on a mode of transport. Figures, being the traveller that I am! Anyway, I pictured him down to a T, from the nose ring in his left nostril, to the tattoos on his left arm (yes okay I clearly have something about the left hand side). He had dark messy hair, chocolate brown eyes. He wore a leather jacket and black jeans, and on some occasions, would appear in a 'beanie hat'. Now, fast forward by only *two weeks* and I had been for coffee with my friend in town. I walked her to the station, and saw her off on her train, and then for some strange reason, instead of taking the *bus* home I decided to take the train. I got my ticket and made a dash for the next one leaving, which was in one minutes time. However, as I made my dash to the platforms, I noticed that there was another one leaving from Platform 3 in a further 3 minutes time. My head told me to take the first one but my Inner Goddess spoke, and told me to take the second, because 3 is my favourite and lucky number. Laughing at the daftness of it all, I strolled down to Platform 3 and jumped onto carriage number 3 almost as if to laugh at myself. The train was full, and so there was no option of seating. It was a rush hour train to London, and I only wanted to go one stop, so I suddenly felt silly for not just taking the previous train, which would have been much quieter with seats. I perched myself against the wall closest to the doorway, and after placing my carrier bags down at my feet, looked up at the face staring back at me. It was HIM. The guy literally from my dreams and visualisations!

Staring at him in disbelief, something even stranger began to happen. I could feel what some may call 'chemistry' swirling in that little space between us, but I liked to think of it as being source energy at play, excited that we were finally in alignment. His eyes locked with mine, and my natural instinct was to look away, but I found myself feeling instantly at ease, and looked right back. At that moment, a lady with a small suitcase on wheels was attempting to squeeze in past us. We both began to smile at the ludicrousness of her refusal to accept that we weren't stood in the doorway for the benefit of our health. I felt like I was caught in a precious moment, but at the same time, was all too aware that in less than eight minutes, I would be getting off at the next stop.

I scanned his body, marvelling at the tattoos, the nose ring, his beanie hat, and the leather jacket in hand. Could it really be, that I had actually visualised my soul mate into my reality? I noticed the ticket in his hand, that stated London Euston as his point of departure and felt saddened that we would soon part company. But as the train pulled into my location, he picked up his bag and stood next to me, waiting to exit. My mind began to work over time, and I panicked. Should I offer him my number? I felt around in my pocket but had no pen on me. Maybe he would talk to me when we got off and were inside the station. The train came to a standstill and he walked slowly behind me, which is when *fear* began to creep in.

'What if he didn't talk to me? Should I be turning around to talk to him? Maybe if I slow down, he will over take me and then the ball is in his court as to whether or not we speak...'

Then the ridiculous thoughts started; 'what if I am imagining all of this anyway? For all I know, he may not even like me. I can't throw myself at some guy that I stood opposite on the train for eight minutes... can I?'

I then noticed that he had overtaken me and was most certainly walking slowly and looking back to see if I was still behind him. Maybe my fear was for nothing. Maybe this was it, my moment had arrived and the man I had been visualising was going to whisk me off into the sunset and... oh okay, at least ask me for my number.

As we approached a fork turning, he slowed right down and let me naturally over take him. I exited down onto the escalator, and then was convinced that he actually must be following me. Again, panic and fear started swirling around my mind and body, and I decided to take a risk. Once I stepped off the bottom stair of the escalator, I walked over to a bench by the bus stop and decided that if he truly wanted to talk to me then he would have the perfect opportunity to come over, sit next to me, and do so.

Looking down at the floor, I decided that I needed to apply a quick coat of lip gloss before I reached the bench in mind, and being distracted in this thought process, I failed to notice that my train guy was heading out of the station exit.

For days after this incident, I could not get him out of my mind. I even went as far as to look at sites on the Internet that specialise in listing what is called 'Missed Connections'. Oh okay, I actually did more than just look, I posted an ad! I was so confused at what this whole thing meant. I was sure, with every fibre in my being, that I had magicked this gorgeous creature, beanie hat and all, into my line of vision. So why, if it was 'meant to be' had we not taken things further?

After a few days of feeling sorry for myself and licking my wounds, it finally dawned on me that I had destroyed the moment, by breaking the connection with source, and my guy, and allowing Fear to take over.

The moral of the story?: In order for the law of attraction to work to its full potential, it is vital that you believe in its ability to do so, 100%. As soon as I started to panic and question, I lost the connections made and the energy level dropped. If I had just listened to my Inner Goddess, and taken that risk and given him my number, things may be very different today. But instead, I let Fear and the Victim take over. This is why it's so important to realise, that listening to your Inner Goddess, and tuning into Source energy is something that needs to be maintained and implemented on a daily basis. It is not something that can be mastered over a short period of time and then that's it, done. It takes daily practise, and should become a crucial part of your routine, as vital as brushing your teeth.

So, have fun, get creative, keep up your visualisations and you never know when your partner may walk into your reality.

On a more practical note, knowing exactly the kind of person that you are hoping to attract, means that you will be more aware of whether or not there is a 'fit' when you do meet someone or start dating. You can weed out the potentials from the no go in a much quicker fashion. Stop dithering around with guys that don't match you, the old saying 'stop trying to fit a square peg into a round hole' actually has a hell of a lot of weight behind it'.

On that note, let's dive right into the weird, the wonderful and the bizarre world of dating.

Love Blossoms – Vixen and Inner Goddess

Loving crack of the whip #18: A date is a simple meeting of two people, to see if there is a 'fit'. If there is not, it is not the end of the world. You would not invest in a dress that was two sizes too small for you so why do so many of us seem that desperate to be in a relationship that we settle for second best? There is a lot of truth in the old saying 'you cannot fit a square peg into a round hole'. You can keep on trying, but if it's not happening, it's not happening. The longer that you spend chasing the wrong guy, the less time you spend with the right guy...

You thought this was about surviving date number one and progressing onto date two, three and four... right?

Before we look at how to have a successful date, it's crucial to look at *who* you are taking out on this date in terms of the role that you shall play for the evening. Are you heading out as your most authentic self or are you caught up in a mass of worry and fear? I want to offer you a little piece of advice before embarking upon any date, but especially that most dreaded first.

Think of a first date as simply being a meeting between two individuals to see if there is a fit. If there is, then it will be felt mutually and things should progress to date two smoothly.

If there is not a fit, then pause, breathe and just be ready to accept, that this particular person is not the best fit for you. It does not mean that the day or evening has been wasted. Go out on a date with an open heart and open mind and see each one as a practise run for the one that will knock your socks off! Even if you realise within minutes of meeting, that this is not the person for you in *love* it does not mean that they may not be great person aligned to you in *life*. Just because you don't see yourself ripping their clothes off and imagine marching them down the aisle, does not mean that the person in front of you is not here for a reason.

I believe that every person we meet in life is a *gift*. Everyone, whether you like them or not, has something to offer you. Even in someone that you claim to hate, is a lesson to be taken. For instance, colliding with what you *don't* want serves as a gentle reminder that you are off your path, and of what you *do* want in life. So don't be too quick to up and leave or feel disappointed if the person you are to spend a few hours with is not the man or woman of your dreams. It is all interconnected and this person is a stepping stone to the next date, the next person and so on. Besides, people are not just there as potential love candidates. You never know who you may meet in terms of fellow creative's , potential employees and last but by no means least, future friends.

So – when going on a date, stop worrying and analysing. Don't project your unrealistic expectations onto the other person. It's not fair and you are bound to come away feeling disappointed. Instead, go with an open mind, start things off on a blank slate and you may just come away pleasantly surprised.

When you go with this frame of mind, you stand a far better chance at them wanting to see you again, because you will be your most authentic self. You will also be relaxed and confident and your mind will be focused in the present moment. When you are focused in the present moment (*in* and not *on*) you are connected to your Inner Goddess and to Source energy and wonderful things can happen. If you are not, then you leave space within which fear, and worry, can breed, and your date winds up sipping wine with a character that they have encountered in a variety of exterior packages – the Victim.

I want to just refer back to the idea of focusing **in** the present moment as opposed to focusing **on** the present moment.

'when you focus on the present moment, you can almost miss the magic of the moment for looking too hard. When you master focusing 'in' the present moment, you become enveloped in the fluidity of the moment – a vital cog in the ever moving and energising Universe, of space and time'.

Stay as relaxed as you can when you are in a moment, because the less you actually think about how you look, how you are acting, what is happening, what is being said, the more chance you stand at simply becoming 'lost in the moment' and this really is when you connect to your Inner Goddess and lose your inhibitions. Stop being a spectator looking at the scenario that you are in and become immersed in it.

With this attitude in mind, your date should be a learning curve, and a worthwhile meeting, whether you end up with a future lover or not. So what do you have to lose? Get out there and get mingling and at all times, stay in the present moment, connected to both your Internal energy (Inner Goddess) and external energy (Source). Of course, a date is not just about how you present yourself in terms of how you are feeling within yourself, but it is the main backbone of success and happiness. I am now going to glide into the other areas of concern that are 'what to wear, body language, flirting and seduction'…

THE VIXEN AND INNER GODDESS – LOVE

Loving crack of the whip #19: *Unless you buy into yourself, then you cannot expect another to.*

I am not going to offer you suggestion of what to wear to knock him dead. Think back to the beginning, where we created your Goddess Vision Board and you will already know exactly how you want to present yourself on a first (or future) date. Remember that sexiness, and seduction does not mean the same as 'sex'. A woman can be sexual without jumping into bed. Sexiness is an attitude. It is a state of mind.

So, with this in mind, go back to your Goddess Vision Board and re-create the mood that you did for your Goddess photo shoot before a big date. You can adapt almost any of the exercises throughout this book, to any situation. Just use your imagination and listen to where your Inner Goddess wants to take you. Conjure up an ambiance that makes you feel powerful and sexy, and follow *this* and not what you *think* you should present yourself like on a first date.

'On a date, you want to present a polished version of your most authentic you. This is what the Vixen is. If you feel most confident in heels, then by all means, wear them, But if you feel sassy in flip flops and jeans, then go for it. This is about being yourself and if your

date cannot embrace YOU then they do not deserve date two.'

However I am often asked what are MY secret weapons for a successful date and I am more than happy to share them with you, so here goes:

- *Clean make-up.... a good base that suits my skin tone, mascara, a little cheek tint and a coat of plumping lip gloss is all that I wear. But my eyes are alluring as I use a false lash effect mascara. This is my signature look – choose one area to accentuate, eyes, or lips and don't over do it.*
- *I often opt for one of two outfits: 1) a cowl neck black knee length dress, simple and classy, with boots or, skinny Jeans, boots, a fitted top or basque with a shirt half buttoned over it and away I go. Both clean, simple but powerful.*
- *Nails are another striking point of mine but I don't like false nails, I prefer black or red polish. Vamp it up!*
- *I always wear baby powder as everyone feels comforted by this scent, and then I splash my perfume (Angel by Thierry Mugler) on my pulse points and neck*
- *Hair is kept natural, mine is long and I wear it straight and down. Guys like the ruffled, what have you been up to look, so forget masses of gel and hair spray.*
- *I always wear a good fitting bra, more often than not it is slightly padded. Not that size matters, but it makes me feel accentuated.*
- *I personally do like a heel, but not so tall that I can't walk with ease. Heels arch our back and bottom out, and men find this attractive. We walk from the hip in heels, and this is extremely womanly and captivating.*

So, those are my tips for dressing on a date. Notice that there is no real cleavage or thigh on display. Men like things being left to their imagination. Just enough curve but no real flesh.

Body language can reveal a lot about how you're feeling on the inside, and I don't want get into that subject in too much depth in this book, but some general tips are:

- *Sit in a relaxed position, but do not slouch*
- *Make good eye contact, but do not stare. This will have you come across as 'slightly deranged' rather than confident.*
- *When you first meet, give him or her a touch on the arm or a kiss on the cheek. Make innocent physical contact right away*
- *Same goes for when you leave*

Conversation, I am not even going to start to tell you what YOU would want to talk about on a date as this goes against the whole idea of listening to your Inner Goddess! Just be yourself, but do stay aware of the balance of the conversation. It is great to be passionate and enthusiastic, but make sure that you spend as much time asking questions and listening to your date as you do talking about yourself.

So, the date is covered, but now I want to look at what to do if things don't go as well as planned. Let's start with that dreaded period, right after a date, when we are waiting to hear from that guy/gal, but... we don't.

'If he /she does not call again then do not judge them. Remember what we said about a date simply being a meeting of two individuals to see if there is a fit? Well

clearly, the other person did not feel that there was, and he or she is entitled to feel that.'

No one else is obliged or responsible for YOUR happiness. No one other than YOU. When you find yourself sliding into 'over analysing' what could have 'gone wrong', or wondering what you could have done better, ask yourself the following question, ' during the date, were you operating from your most authentic self? Did you remain open minded and relaxed, and listen to your Inner Goddess?' If the honest answer is yes, then no matter how much you liked this person, you simply were not suited in terms of energy and the only option to make things work would be to completely change who *you* are, in order to better suit *their* needs. And why on earth, if you are the sort of woman who has bought this book, and wants to Unleash her Inner Goddess, would you ever want to do that again?

If you were not yourself during the date then there is very little point in beating yourself up about it. Like I have said before, none of us are perfect, and remaining in connection to your Inner Goddess and Source takes daily practise. Think back to what I said about 'dropping your baggage at the door'. Mistakes happen in life, and the best that we can do, is to learn and grow from them. Rather than sit back, adopting the role of the Victim, just take it as part of a learning curve and admire yourself for having the balls to get out there and actually give it a go in the dating world... it's a cut throat market. Remember that 'what you focus on grows' so do not spend another moment wondering 'what if'. It is what it is and by focusing more on what you do want, and what you would like to happen on your next date with someone, you will be inviting such experiences into your life.

So, you have had the second, third and fourth date, but what happens when you are in a 'relationship' and things sometimes get a little rocky?

Firstly, let's pick out several scenarios that could be defined as rocky, when it comes to love and dating. Things that spring to mind are issues of trust and jealousy, friends – especially female friends, and what to do if your partner is not fulfilling your needs. I will also include the sensitive topics of cheating/affairs and physical and mental abuse.

So – in a nutshell, if you are secure in yourself, and are touching base with your Inner Goddess as you glide through your relationship, in an ideal world, you would not experience things such as jealousy or feeling threatened by other women. But of course, none of us are perfect, and this just a learning curve and part of a life long journey. So let's imagine that you, yes you, right this very minute, are feeling the wrath of the green eyed monster. We have all experienced it at some time or other, and it's the worst emotion, as it can become all consuming. You almost feel as though you are being suffocated by its presence, it is there day and night.

What would you say, is the worst thing about feeling this emotion? I would say, that it is the unpredictability of it. From my own experience, I have *reacted* when jealous, rather than *acted*. It digs at you to your core, and produces this wild, knee jerk reaction, that again, is based on Fear (also anger). Knowing what we know now, would you ever give jealousy the same power that it maybe had in your past? Let's look at it logically together now.

If Fear is the main catalyst behind Jealousy, we immediately want to neutralise its power, because we know, that Fear is a short hop, skip and a jump to becoming the Victim. If and when we feel jealous, we are actually being *controlled* by this powerful emotion. Don't get me wrong, sometimes, jealousy is actually our Inner Goddess trying to communicate with us, and tell us that actually, our gut feeling is spot on, and if we investigate further, we find that actually, our partner does like this other person, and is maybe even having an affair with them.

It is not always wrong to listen to Fear. But you will know, if you are truly honest with yourself, whether or not the Fear that you are feeling, is your Inner Goddess trying to tell you something (women's intuition is amazingly accurate most of the time) or you simply exaggerating things in your imagination and panicking over nothing.

Let's look in more detail at a scenario, that happened to my friend Jane (name changed). Jane had gone out with the girls for a bite to eat, and had missed her boyfriend so much, that she called him to tell him, but he didn't pick up. As she laughed on the outside at the group conversation, inside, she was tossing and turning, her mind working over time. Where was he? He had told her that he would stay in all afternoon and he hoped that she had a great time. Five minutes later, she tried again, and this time, he picked up! But instead of hearing his genuine concern that she was calling when out for lunch and now *he* was convinced that something was wrong with her .. all Jane could focus on was the female voice that was in the background. 'Who's there? I thought you were staying home? Where are you?' Before she knew it, the questions were becoming more and more panicky, and it was clear that Jane was being driven by Fear, and not her Inner Goddess. After accusing him of being out with another woman, Ben finally got a word in edge ways, and told her that he was actually at her Mums place, because he had gone round there to do their lawn like he had promised weeks ago and figured that now would be a good time to do it as the weather was the best that it had been in weeks...

Sadly, when jealousy and fear kick in, their effects are instantaneous, and often, our damage control button seems to somehow not function. If only there was a safety device that would kick in before the words come out of our mouths, but the thing with fear, especially when it turns into jealousy, is that it is a little like a runaway train. As soon as it leaves the station, it races downhill, with no concept of how to break. It's only usually when a huge amount of damage has been done, and we are sat in a crumpled heap amongst the ruins, that we are able to see things with clarity, and by then, it is often too late.

So – you are wondering, well this is all very well, but how can I get my damage control button working next time I feel the overbearing sensation of fear turning into jealousy?

Well, to be honest with you, this particular scenario will involve some pro-active ass kicking on your part. Only YOU can master this emotion. But if you want to do it, then you can and will.

Kicking ass – Jealousy / Fear

Loving crack of the whip#20: *Jealousy comes from FEAR of not being good enough. If you believe that you are not good enough then you are choosing to play the Victim. The number one reason for relationship breakdowns, is Jealousy and lack of trust. It is a self fulfilling prophecy. Why bother? You will wind up driving your partner away anyway – so ask yourself, is this actually what you want? Do you want to drive them away so that you can tell yourself that old tale of how 'this always happens to me, I am doomed when it comes to love'? Maybe it feels safe to be the Victim ?*

In quite simple terms, an effective way to kick the ass of jealousy, is to imagine, like you did with your Inner Goddess, as a cartoon character. Personalise it and visualise it. Think of it as being the devilish character and know, that it is powerful, but also toxic. You need to blast this little fella out of the equation as soon as possible, because he multiplies rapidly, with one goal in mind, and that is to sabotage your happiness, but also, to attack your Inner Goddess.

When you are operating from your authentic self, and are in touch with your Inner Goddess, you ooze self confidence. You know, that there is no place for Jealousy and Fear in your love life, because you are all too aware, that when you maintain your optimum energy levels, and give out good vibrations, you will be in perfect alignment with those that are supposed to share your life. The energy between you and your partner will be so electric that they would not want to look elsewhere anyway, but if they did/do, then they were not actually the right match for you. At least not if you were emitting your most authentic self/energy that is.

it's a vicious cycle really – if you are not feeling at your best, and are swaying more to the Victim zone, than you are Vixen with Inner Goddess, then you can't expect to keep your partner connected to you with your self created energy anyway. Because you will have taken yourself out of that zone, out of that bubble, and this in turn, invites fear and other negative energies and emotions in.

So – in order to keep Fear and Jealousy away, visualise yourself and your partner together, in a protective bubble created by the sun or moons rays. Imagine that energy, penetrating yourself, to the core, and in turn, connecting (like a rainbow) to your partner's heart chakra. Focus on the giving and receiving of the powerful love energy that is being generated and whipped up between you. Focus on this and not the feelings aroused within you of fear and jealousy. In doing this, you will be zoning in on the positive vibration and this in itself, gives no room for the manifestation of the negative.

Then, as an addition, you can imagine the characters of fear and jealousy as being outside of your protective self generated bubble. Think of your energy field as being a little like an electric fence. Every time they attempt to force their way into the bubble, they are catapulted backwards, yelping from the zap that your energy has given them. At all times, remember that YOU are in control of fuelling or not fuelling the spark of jealousy, so stay vigilant and refuse to let it get out of control.

Before I move away from this topic, I do want to quickly refer back to the part where I mentioned that sometimes, Jealousy and fear arise because our Inner Goddess is actually speaking the truth and is trying to alert us to something. So how do we handle this sort of situation, if we are not yet sure that our Inner Goddess is correct, and we also don't want our feelings to spiral out of control?

Well, the best thing to do, is to **write a letter to your Inner Goddess.** Yep, actually sit down with paper and a pen, or your laptop if you are more of typist, and write a letter to your Inner Goddess. Imagine that your Inner Goddess is a friend, who has been trying to tell you something for a while now, and you have finally agreed to hear her out. Explain to her that you understand that she feels x,y and z, and then tell her what your take on the matter is. Ask her what is it that supports her opinion? Can she back it up with any evidence? Then, you guessed it, you are going to wait a little while, and then respond as your Inner Godess and speak from her point of view. If it helps, create that separate email inbox, and label it as Inner Goddess in your contacts, and then you can actually physically send an email to your Inner Goddess, and open it yourself a few hours later, read it, and respond.

This exercise will get you looking at things from an external/spectator perspective, and compare what your heart and head are telling you. Have a frank discussion with yourself and look at things rationally, before diving in with both feet. Keep in mind the character of Jealousy and Fear, and if necessary, also do the technique above, where you visualise yourself in the bubble with your partner. If after all of this rational and positive thinking, you are still being guided by your Inner Goddess, then by all means, do go ahead and see where she takes you. But at least you will be able to say, if things do backfire, that you did what your Inner Goddess told you, and *acted* rather than *reacted.*

Of course, sometimes, our Goddess is unfortunately correct, and relationships break down, because the jealousy actually was founded. So what is the best way to handle such a situation, as a Vixen in tune with her Inner Goddess, rather than having a negative life experience drag you back into the Victim zone.

Inner Goddess tackles a broken heart

Loving crack of the whip #21: A broken heart sucks. I am not going to convince you of otherwise. But the positive is that, in order to feel such immense pain, you must have experienced love – and to love is a sign of letting go of fear and taking a dive into the Ocean. Each time that you get washed back to shore, swim back out with purpose. Staying put on the sideline is simply not an option. The waves of life will take you, sooner rather than later. So isn't it better to choose your direction, than be swept out like washed up garbage?

This section is actually applicable to a broken heart and spirit, due to any reason. It could be due to an affair, but let's face it, a broken heart, for whatever reason, is never a nice experience.

Most of us will be familiar with that old Whitney Houston song *'where do broken hearts go?'* I like to think that your broken heart does not go anywhere. It simply repairs itself over time, and remains as part of the colourful tapestry of your unique and precious heart. A little like a broken leg, the tissue knits itself back together, and sure, there may be a little scarring, and you may have to go easy on your heart for a while, but over time, things strengthen again and you put the broken bone down to life experience.

The best way to deal with a broken heart, is to just give yourself permission to 'be' with it for a little while.Don't listen to that age old advice of 'get over it'. I have already covered what I think of that line. Rather than get over it, get on with it. Befriend your broken heart, and acknowledge its presence. Jumping into bed with anyone, drinking Vodka, and binging on ice cream will only leave you with regret, a hangover, and a bigger waistline. You simply cannot deny or ignore that gnawing feeling, so 'feel and heal' it.

The Feel and Heal technique

This technique is simple, yet effective. It is something that I use frequently with clients who come to me in order to get over a broken heart. I again, advise creating a brand new email address. You can get these free with hotmail, yahoo, gmail and so on. Name the address as the person who hurt you and then whenever you start to feel things – and possibly want to tell them exactly how you feel (ouch, don't do it!), you can let it all out in an email to this fabricated person.

I believe that letting it out in this way is healthy, because you are able to articulate and express how you are feeling, whilst limiting any damage that can be done from reacting to surges of emotion by mailing or calling your ex. You get to 'let it all out' but it's kept between just you and yourself. Keeping the emails in this secret inbox also means that you can go back over what you have written when you are feeling a little better. Over time, you will see just how far you have actually come, and may even raise a smile at some of the material that you produced when *reacting.*

'After any sort of heartache, I recommend giving yourself 'space' for a period of 21 days before acting upon anything'.

Why? Well, remember that 'it takes 21 days to make or break a habit'.

In 21 days, you can spend time working on yourself as opposed to trying to change the other person's point of view. Most people, when breaking up with someone ask for a period of space. Even if they still have feelings for the other party, the fact that things have come to breaking point often means that things cannot go on as they are, and something needs to give. Often, we **fear** giving someone space, incase they happen to 'forget about us' during our absence. Either that, or meet someone else. But think about it logically – when you have dated someone, or just known someone, whether the outcome was good or bad, have you simply forgotten about them in as little as 21 days? Of course not! And to be blunt, if he or she *can* forget you in as little as three weeks, then they didn't deserve to have you in the first place and it is better that you find that out sooner rather than later.

You are granting yourself time within which to digest what has happened, and begin to work out how you feel, with *clarity*.

Often, when we are first presented with the loss of another, we react to the panic and fear of the prospect of losing that person from our lives forever, and being alone.

Give yourself time within which to work out how you truly feel – act rather than react. Turning into an emotionally loose cannon and chasing after someone who is clearly wanting to separate themselves from you (whether for good, or just the time being) will only drive them further away from you.

Besides, it's essential, in these 21 days, that you preserve your sense of self, and connect with your Inner Goddess, before you slide into the role of the Victim, as a broken heart is a specifically vulnerable time that may give rise to such an occurrence. When I say 'don't play the Victim', I do not mean that you are not allowed to be upset. But know, that just because you are hurting right now, and missing someone you have loved, the following aspects still exist in regards to your sense of self/individuality:

You were an individual in your own right before you connected with this other person and you are still that same individual right now, only more evolved from knowing them. Even if things have gone horribly wrong, look at what you can take from the relationship and use as experience. Remember what I said about first dates – never regret meeting and communicating with another individual. Through experiencing the negative, what we don't want, or heartache, we are pushed closer towards something or someone that will work for us.

Remember that **'you cannot alter the direction of the wind, but you can always adjust your sails'**. No matter how much you hurt right now, you will cope, because that's what us women (and humans) do! You can choose how this experience affects you. Remember the Law of Attraction, 'what you focus on, grows'. Rather than focus on the events that led up to the heartbreak, focus on how you'd like your tomorrow to be and look ahead rather than back.

Talk to your Inner Goddess and make sure that she stays in

vision. In staying in tune with her, you will remain on track to whatever is next in store for you on your personal journey. When we are not in touch with our Inner Goddess, and are not our most authentic self, we can veer off course, and find ourselves in all kinds of unhealthy situations.

Don't let an already sad situation spiral out of control – you cannot change what has happened, but you can influence your tomorrow. In letting negative emotion and energy drown you, you soon find yourself lost in the world of the Victim. Once here, things snowball out of control. Negativity breeds negativity and the law of attraction will give you more of this existence unless you take back control of shaping and creating your future. Grab this by the balls and thank your lucky stars for being alive and having had the opportunity to experience love!

Sometimes, it's hard though – if you are caught up in a relationship that seems impossible to let go of. Especially if it is one of abuse. Often, we can lose our sense of self because we have invested so much into another person, that things (energy) becomes dangerously unbalanced, and we are actually 'drained'. Once in this position, it's even harder to just snap back into our 'Vixen/Inner Goddess' role. Sometimes, no matter how much we 'know' that we are playing the role of the Victim, it just feels almost impossible to reconnect with our Inner Goddess.

Let me tell you a secret – I was once a Victim. For seven years. I lost myself totally – but here I am today. If I had not found myself in that position, and had my heart ripped out and stomped upon, I would not have had the privilege of spending the next five years discovering myself. Oh I know – that sounds so… cliche. But I can honestly say, hand on heart, that I do not regret my life as it has panned out so far one little bit. The journey of discovering and connecting to my own Inner Goddess was a period of growth that I may never repeat again in this lifetime.

Of course, I miss my ex from time to time, and wish that I could have done things differently (I cringe when I look at how insecure I once was!). But again, if I had been the person I am now, back then, well I would not be sat here today writing this book. Remember, that sometimes, life has something in store for us, that we cannot yet see. Just because you cannot yet see the 'light at the end of the tunnel', does not mean that there is not an extremely bright and vibrant light burning away in the distance. But without experiencing the darkness, we would not appreciate the light.

'In your darkest hour, you will find gold'

When all seems hopeless, and you feel that the dark period is never ending, don't be in such a hurry to be magically healed. Look for the potential lessons that could be waiting for you to discover like hidden treasure in the darkness. The sooner that you find the clues, the quicker you reach the treasure. Trust me, we all have hidden treasure chests waiting.

Of course, love is not the only area that we may need advice in. In a modern day Vixen's life, it can be hard to keep your cool when it comes to other areas too, such family, friends and career.

I am going to begin by grouping family and friends together, and look at relationships that are important to you, but are not with those who you'd class as a partner or lover. Who are we left with? Friends, family and work colleagues (for most of us.)

The first thing that I want to look at, is how we often listen too much to the opinion of those close to us, over the opinion of our Inner Goddess. I for one, used to be guilty of this very issue. I spent most of my early twenties approaching a situation in the following fashion:

1 I would ask myself how I felt about it and what did I think was best to do? (note that I say 'what was best to do' rather than 'what I wanted to do').
2 I would then question my initial conclusion several times before moving onto step 3
3 I would call my Mum and ask her advice. Secretly hoping for confirmation that my decision was correct
4 Whether she agreed or not, I would feel that I somehow needed to double check, so would then ask several close friends what they thought and…

The cycle would continue over and over until finally, I either did what my original idea was but it was far too late, or I had got myself so wound up, that I reacted rather than acted, and somehow the whole thing (whatever the thing was) was blown out of all proportion and I adopted the Victim role and swore that I would never consider a, b or c again.

But the real drama and issue, was not the decision under scrutiny, but was actually the sad fact that I felt the need to ask every man and his dog what they thought that I should do.

Why is it that so many of us do this? Is it really because we want confirmation, or is it that we *fear* making a decision that may ultimately lead us to lose something or someone that we want to have?

Never forget, that when you are operating from your most authentic self, you will draw those most suited to you into your energy field, and they will remain there naturally, because there is the best fit. If someone or something, is not intended for us, then no matter how hard we try, we will always wind up losing it at some point along the way, because the Universe knows what suits us better than we sometimes know ourselves. So with this in mind, just try trusting in your intuition a little more. Listen to your Inner Goddess, and then take a chance, and instead of asking for everyone Else's validation, trust your own life choices, and stick with them. For as long as you can do this, you may not get the outcome that you think you want, but will get something better.

Besides, however hard it may seem at the actual time, if you are honest with yourself, would you really want to keep someone or something in your life, if they were not truly suited to your most authentic self?

If you choose to chase things that are not truly matched to you and your life path, then you are inviting and prolonging the agony of feeling disconnected from your Inner Goddess. Most discord in relationships comes about from something not quite sitting right with your Inner Goddess. There is a miss match, a misalignment, and in your heart of hearts, in your subconscious mind, you are aware of this. Have you ever been in a relationship with someone, and wanted to keep hold of them, but somehow, you know it's not right, and although on the outside, you 'appear' to be fighting to keep hold of what you claim to want, you have this bizarre internal battle, between clinging onto something (fear of loss) and letting things go and work out for your higher good? Note how I linked the wanting to control things as being linked to Fear again? Yes, it really does control us and our actions more than we realise.

'But be aware, that when you are stuck in such a situation, you always have the choice to change it. Have a little more faith in yourself. Remember that whatever the outcome, you really will be okay. You will be just fine, even if you wind up alone! (which rarely happens to most of us – again, that is just another cruel story of 'what if' that is invented by fear).'

Don't let fear turn you into a Victim, and keep you stuck in situations that are not best suited to you. It is inevitable that they will come to an end sooner or later. Isn't it better to face the fear of change head on, and move forwards towards your true destiny, in tune with your Inner Goddess? The longer you drag out being in the wrong place, the longer you will wait to find yourself in the right place and although it takes courage to jump into the Ocean of life and trust that it will take you to where you want to go, the rewards of actually living the life most suited to YOU is priceless.

You can't please everyone – put yourself first

Loving crack of the whip #22: *If you are constantly putting the needs of others ahead of those of your own, ask yourself why. Are you acting from a place of unconditional love or are you acting in response to insecurity, and fear of not being accepted? If it is the latter then you are simply choosing the Victim! If it is the former, then give yourself a break – giving out more than what you have is short changing the ones you care for, and don't you ALL deserve the best?*

Talking about our relationships with others, the next thing that comes to mind, is how so many of ladies can devote more time and attention on those around us, often, at the expense of our own emotional welfare. I for one, am known amongst my friends, as being the one who they can turn to at any time, day or night, for advice. I think that this is great, I am of course, humbled by their trust in me. If I keep it in balance, then it is great and rewarding to feel that I can inspire someone in this life time. But there have been times when I have given more energy out than what I actually had stored. This is when problems can arise.

Firstly, I began to feel drained, and realised that I was not functioning at the best of my ability. I then became irritable, and sleepless nights followed. As a result of sleepless nights, stress crept in, and I then began to resent the person responsible for 'sucking me dry'. That may sound a little harsh, but there is no time for me to sugar coat things. I felt used. Like I had been sucked up and spat out and left to dry in the harsh sunlight. But how could I blame anyone else but myself? I was the one who had given too much. I was responsible for maintaining my personal energy levels and I had neglected to do so.

YOU are responsible for maintaining your own personal energy levels, and you cannot blame anyone else if you find yourself run ragged.

You are not responsible for the health and happiness for everyone else around you. They are responsible for themselves. Sure, we can be there for others, and I advocate living life with an open heart. I am not even close to suggesting that you start to become 'selfish'. But taking care of your own needs before others, is not selfish. It can actually benefit those around you.

Think of yourself like the finest car, motorbike, whatever you prefer to imagine. You would not top up a Ferrari for example, with the minimum amount of the cheapest fuel on the market, and then expect it to get you from one end of the country to the other. Would you? No. So why are YOU any different? Now if you just said 'I am not', let me just point out that you actually are, you are far more precious than any vehicle in the world. So treat yourself with the respect to match that.

Now, the more energy that you can conserve, the more you quality energy you can give out to others. When you run yourself ragged, and are spreading yourself too thinly, you are only able to offer the bare minimum to others. But when you take better care of yourself first, not only will you feel healthier, happier, and in tune with your Inner Goddess, and Source energy, you will then be able to give more back out.

Think back to the exercise where you felt yourself being recharged by the sun or the moon, and you then visualised yourself stood in unison with your partner. Remember the giving and receiving of energy – the constant flow, back and forth. The energy, with all of this movement, was stimulated and whipped up into a mixture of two streams of energy. This together, became an unstoppable force. Well, visualise yourself with that same rainbow of energy. But this time, feel the rainbow take on a life of its own. Imagine the rays, pulsing not only outwards, but also inwards. Racing through your veins, like a warm stream of anaesthesia. The colourful flow fills up every inch of your body, and you feel almost intoxicated by its presence. When you begin to feel yourself giving too much to others, take a step back and picture this scenario.

Allow your energy to turn inwards and take care of you first, and then meditate (maybe before bed) being on your own hilltop, taking in the sun or moons energy. Let the Source fill you up and recharge you and know, that you are safe to take this space. You would not call a mobile phone a 'failure' because it needed to take overnight to be charged would you? So why think any less of yourself? The main reason that women (men too, but women in particular) feel that they are selfish for putting their own needs above others, is because we have come from generations of women who adhered to being 'the perfect housewife, mother' , the whole package. There has been this self created pressure – those chains that I referred to in section one. As soon as you give yourself permission to top up your own energy levels, you choose to refuse to chain yourself up in unrealistic expectations and ideals. You choose to shun the emotion of Guilt that accompanies the idea of taking better care of yourself. Guilt is on the same wavelength as fear – we do not want or need it. It is one of the main culprits found in that backpack of baggage that we disposed of in Section Two -. Guilt, just like fear, gets along best with the role of the Victim. Picture guilt as a character, just like you did with fear, and next time you feel it, imagine it being zapped by your protective energy bubble.

Choose to nourish your Inner Goddess. Choose to top up your energy resources on a daily basis. Don't wait until the tank is half empty, make sure that the tank is overflowing! That way, you can give more quality time and energy to those closest to you on a daily basis.

There is nothing wrong in drawing a few lines in the sand. Perhaps think about:

- *Allocating a slot into your daily or weekly routine for chatting with family and friends. Stick within this boundary*
- *When you begin a phone call, explain to whoever is on the other end, that you only have 15, 20, 45 minutes, because you are then doing a, b or c*
- *If the phone rings and you are relaxing or doing something for yourself, then let it go to answerphone. If it's a matter of life or death, they will leave a message and you can call them right back.*
- *Make time in your daily schedule for some 'me time', whether it be watching TV, a bubble bath, cooking or creating.*

Which leads me onto my next subject, that is how Unleashing your Inner Goddess may rub a few people around you up the wrong way.

People are creatures of habit: and a lot of people are not all that keen on change. The fact that you picked up this book, and are close to the end of it, shows that you are someone who is looking to improve their personal energy, and enhance your life experience. I am not comparing people here – those who seek and look to grow are not 'above' those who choose not to. We all have a choice. I did not begin my spiritual journey until the age of twenty five, but I was no less a person aged twenty four. I was just in a different place at that time. And now, looking back, I can say that those years leading up to my twenty fifth were all gearing me up to something bigger. I had to go through things at my own pace, in my own time, because there were lessons for me to learn before I could develop my own spiritual standpoint.

So if you find yourself frustrated, as you attempt to explain a philosophy or theory to someone close to you but they don't seem to want to get it, remember, that they are exactly where *they* need to be right now, in terms of their own spiritual journey. Maybe it is not time for them to learn certain things just yet, because they have to go through a, b or c in order to discover it for themselves. Or, maybe they are going to be blessed with their own philosophy, and simply on their own journey, and the Universe is directing them to that.

Do be aware, that when you begin to relax, centre yourself and tune into your Inner Goddess on a more frequent basis, there will be a shift in your energy field. Friends and family may (or may not) pick up on this and to begin with, it could be slightly unsettling for them. Remember, that when one person presents a change, it holds a mirror up to those around them. They begin to question their own lives, and if they are not a point where they are ready or willing to take a spiritual journey, then they may feel resentful of you for probing them – even though they are actually probing themselves. It's sad but true, that sometimes, friends even accuse you of having 'changed' in a negative way, and withdraw themselves from the friendship. Seriously! – when I began my journey of Unleashing my Inner Goddess, and working with the law of attraction, a 'dark natured' friend of mine, who was actually comfortable and secure in her daily depression told me that it would be better if we cut contact, because I was 'too happy' for her. I presented answers to everything but she did not want to hear them. She was not questioning. She was quite happy to remain unhappy, because her fear of change and being happy actually scared her more.

But it all depends doesn't it – on where your friends are at in their personal life journeys. You may find, that the women in your life are intrigued by your new found confidence and peace. Remember that Goddess energy, is interconnected with Universal energy, therefore, we all give and receive a shared energy. The more of us who can connect to the present and focus on keeping this energy positive and raised, the bigger the global effect. If you have friends who you think would be interested in joining you on your journey, then pass this info on to them. Friends can take things to a whole other level, and can be a great support network in times of need. Something as simple as having a friend who completes the 21 day programme at the same time as you can keep you motivated when the chips are down. Writing down points that inspire you and giving them to your friend (and vice versa) means that she can remind you of these when the Victim comes knocking. One popular past time for women the world over, is 'book club'. Why not gather a few of you together and read this book as your chosen material? Perhaps those in the group would not otherwise have been led to this material, but this could be a good way to introduce it. Besides, within a group, you can create a wonderfully charged energy and gain strength and inspiration from *each other.*

You know when I feel inwardly beautiful? When I am with my girlfriends and we are having a 'goddess circle' – Jennifer Aniston

So one last piece of advice that I want to offer you is:

This journey is something personal, to you. Do not worry about what others think, because as a Vixen in tune with her Inner Goddess, you know now that you do not need to seek out the approval of others. If this book has in some way, helped you feel more centred and enlightened, then great! But my main aim has been to give you a gentle reminder, that you are great just as you are, and if you just listen to yourself and trust in yourself, then life will unfold exactly as it should.

It has been a pleasure to share this short amount of time with you, existing in the warm depths of your mind. I know, that I can bid you farewell,safe in the knowledge that you will never be alone. For as long as you are living and breathing, you will always have the unconditional love, support, and guidance of the best friend you will ever have – your Inner Goddess! And should you ever feel like you are losing sight of her, and are veering towards the role of the Victim, just pick up this book and pick a page, any page, and I guarantee that you will instantly feel better. Above all, enjoy your life from this day forward. Unlock your hidden desires, create the life intended for you. It's already out there waiting… you just need to get your heels on and seduce it into your corner.

Love, Angela

THE HIDDEN BUT NOT SO HIDDEN SECTION OF THE INNER GODDESS AS A SEXUAL ENTITY.

I do hope that you haven't flicked to the end section of this book before reading the other sections first. Why do I ask that? Because it is the exact thing that I would do.

I wanted to keep this topic separate because this book's main principle is to look at becoming grounded, comfortable in your own skin, in tune with your personal energy, and also that of the Universe, and as a result, this will of course enhance all areas of your life, especially in regards to the love area. I looked a little at love in section three, but now I want to look at sexuality and the art of seduction in more depth. I wanted to keep it separate though, because I didn't want this book to become sexually themed or laced, as I want the main message throughout to become Universal. Not all women have an interest in all things sexual. Some are very happy as they are, and some are not sexually inclined at all. I did not want the concept of the Inner Goddess to become too wrapped up with women being seen as sexual objects. At the same time, I do not want sexuality and sex to become taboo, because it is a natural extension of self expression, and an area that we all have a right to feel liberated in. If after reading this far, you still want to accompany me into the weird and wonderful world of the Goddess and Sexuality, then please, do proceed further.

Let's begin, by looking at why sexuality, sensuality, seduction and erotica, are areas that so many of us often feel threatened by. A few suggestions are as follows:

We think that we are not SEXY, therefore, how can we play the part? How can we convince another that we are sexy, sexual, how can we seduce, if we cannot even seduce ourselves?

We come from generations of women who were raised to believe that feeling and acting sexual and seductively was not a *ladylike thing to do.*

Society, the media, often criticises women solely based upon their appearance and if a woman is overtly sexual, then this can be branded as 'slutty'

There are so many mixed messages about what it means to be sexy and to seduce – so many 'rules' that we are supposed to follow in order to get that guy/gal

Because it appears to be such an exclusive club, we worry – 'what if I don't get the guy/gal, what if I am useless in bed'…

Now, all of the above statements/issues are based upon our old chums Fear and Guilt. Guilt plays a big role when it comes to letting our hair down and 'going with the flow' as a sexual, sensual, erotic woman.

Let's break things down into sections or topics, and we will start with 'Just what *is* sexy?'

Just what is sexy?
Before I discuss this, I want you to write, in a short sentence, Sexy is

....

....

For me, I would have to say 'Sexy is being alive in your own skin'.

Look at the statement that you have written and ask yourself, do you think that it is realistic, and does it apply to YOU?

Now, I want you to think back, without thinking too intensely, to a time when you felt really sexy. Describe it, a time when you were totally at ease. No one else but you needs to know. Feel free to jot it down or simply recall it in your mind, but close your eyes and visualise the experience. What were you wearing? Who were you with? Where were you? What scents/sounds/tastes/other sensual memories do you recall? Be aware of how this visualisation exercise affects your heart rate, your pulse, your mood, your emotions and your body language. Report any other physical sensations, such as arousal.

Now, sum up that memory in five adjectives. If possible try and apply the adjectives to how YOU were feeling.

Now, I want you to think of a time in your life, where you felt 'un-sexy'. Perhaps it was on a night out, where you didn't feel comfortable with how you looked, or maybe it was a disaster with a partner, and it was their opinion that affected the way that you felt. Do the same as you did above, and visualise this moment. Really put yourself back into the memory, as if it were happening again, right now. Notice – what changes take place in your physical and emotional state as you do this? Compare with visualisation number one. Jot this down.

Again, sum up this experience in five adjectives.

From participating in this little exercise, I hope that you will have perhaps noticed some things about yourself.For example:

How much of your positive and negative experience was linked to your looks/self image/self confidence?
To what extent did childhood memories/guilt/religion/societies moralistic values affect how you felt?

What role did your partner (if present) play a role in your experience/mood?

Now answer honestly, with the new attitude that I hope that this journey has and is given/giving you, if you were to experience a similar event now, would you handle things in the same way?

I now want to talk a little bit about looks, and how you feel about your body, in a more sexual way.

Let's be honest here, it's not something that the majority of us discuss over lunch with our mothers, friends is it? We all have hang ups with ourselves, especially naked. So right here, right now, let's tackle some of that unspoken 'stuff' and see if we can put your mind at rest.

Do I look good naked?

The truth is, **nobody** in the world can answer that question honestly. Why? Well, it would simply be that one persons opinion. Opinions are not facts, and opinions can and do change.

The only person who can and should answer such a question, is yourself. Same goes for other questions, like 'am I sexy? am I attractive? ' and so on.

There is not one definition in the entire Universe that says 'sexy is..., beauty is...,'. Who, just *who* is it who defines such things?

YOU.

It's all about perception and belief. The old cliche 'beauty is in the eye of the beholder' is spot on. But the only eyes that should matter, when it comes to self definition, are yours. let's be frank here, if you seek validation from external sources, you are only going to be disappointed. Human nature changes, it is fluid, and you may be the hottest thing to someone one month, and the next month, they claim that they find your repulsive. But this does not mean that you *are* repulsive. That is simply their opinion.

This all sounds like such obvious advice, I know – but be honest... we have ALL allowed some exes cruel remarks damage how we feel about ourselves haven't we? We all seek approval from those around us. We may not realise we do it, but we do.

But relate this issue back to our three roles: The Victim, The Vixen and the Inner Goddess. If you allow your life, your self image, your mood, be determined by the attitudes and beliefs of others, which role are you adhering to? The Victim! Worrying what others think, seeking approval, and looking to 'fit in' to what society has led you to believe is the acceptable, is behaviour fuelled by FEAR. It is all a figment of your imagination, all an illusion. You see, no two people will see the same person, the same naked body (or clothed body) and think the same thing. Even you may look in the mirror and see something totally different to the reality, and there is an actual condition called 'body dysmorphia', where sufferers believe that they have physical flaws that only they can see. Just think about Anorexia, Bulimia – it's all blown out of proportion in the mind. Therefore, only we can gain control of what goes on in our mind. Only we can alter our perception of self. You could spend your whole life striving for the 'perfect' body, and then lose it all in an instant. Nothing stays the same, nothing lasts forever, our bodies change on a daily basis. Make the best of what you have got, sure. Our bodies are a beautiful blessing. But relax – true beauty really does come from the inside out.

You actually have total control over how you feel about your own body, sexiness is a state of mind, so think yourself sexy!

Thinking yourself sexy, now that you are used to carrying out visualisation exercises throughout this book, should come naturally. You know, that 'what you focus on grows' in terms of your immediate thoughts, and on a grander scale (the law of attraction). What can be a tiny physical flaw, could be blown out of all proportion. How many friends do you have, who constantly ask you 'am I fat?' ,but you *honestly* think that they have nothing to worry about and tell them that it is all in their imagination. *Has it ever occurred to you, that you may be one of 'those' annoying friends yourself?'* Even if you do think/feel it, keep it to yourself, because people are easily convinced of things if they hear them often enough. Stop being your own worst enemy, and be kinder to yourself.

Let me tell you a little true story – I had a few blackheads, one day in my twenties. But the more that I stared at my face in the mirror, the worse the problem *appeared* to be. Deciding that they simply must be removed, I began to squeeze viciously, relieved as the offending dried sebum wiggled its way out of the blocked pore. The next morning, I woke, to find large red, inflamed spots, where the blackheads had once been. All of that squeezing had 'upset' my fragile pale skin, and it had reacted in self defence accordingly. I can see this now, but at the time, in my mind, the blackheads has been the first warning sign that this terrible curse of acne was about to plague my life. 'I have acne' I hollered, and continued to stare at my reflection in the mirror, morning and night for the next few years! I bought this cream and that cream, I over applied everything, totally drying my face out, which in turn created even more 'acne', until finally, I took myself along to see my Doctor, who prescribed antibiotics, to finally clear my self created mess up.

But the 'mental' scarring from such an affliction, as those of you who suffered with it, lasts a life time. During those years, I had lost friends, dates, even a job – all through a low self confidence, and resorting to days where I simply hid in my house, because I could not get past the mirror from drowning in my pool of self loathing.

Looking back at it now, with clarity, I feel sorry for the younger version of me, as I know the pain that she suffered. But I am also a little angry. If I had just treated the blackheads with the attention that they deserved, I would have most likely never have blown (literally) my face up out of all proportion. Like so many body issues, it was a self perpetuating, vicious cycle. Stress exacerbates acne, so the more that I meddled, and worried about it, the more that I *created* the acne.

Take a moment now, and be honest with yourself – do you have any body issues, that you could be making worse through the power of your mind? Have you blown the whole thing out of proportion? There are so many examples, there are those of us who fixate on our weight, become so down about it, and start comfort eating. This then piles on the pounds, and we say 'see, I told you I need to lose weight!'. It is almost like we have something else going on inside, a deeper rooted unhappiness, and so we look for external things to zone in on, something to point the finger at for being the cause of our low self esteem. But why do this? Isn't it quite simply, a tragic case of self sabotage?

Self Sabotage is behaviour associated with a feeling of not being good enough, not worthy. On some level, we truly believe that we do not deserve happiness

Look at that statement again, and it now becomes crystal clear obvious just what is really the underlying cause of the majority of our body issues.

Guilt, Fear, Worry – all behaviours that we are now trying to avoid, because if we allow them to control us, then we are once again, choosing to play the role of the Victim. Okay, so until you become aware of behaviour patterns, and break them down, it isn't all that clear. But now that you do know, how are you going to tackle any issues that you may have? How are you going to address your image, your body image, your sexiness, now that you are more aware of your Inner Goddess, and her need to exist in a state that is not governed by negative dominant and destructive emotion? Only YOU can change how YOU see yourself, and at the end of the day, that is what it comes down to. YOU.

If you re-programme your subconscious mind, and give yourself permission to just relax and be comfortable in your own skin, then everything else, your ability to feel attractive, sexy, sensual, will all follow suit.

Once you are feeling more confident in your own skin, true magic begins to happen. You will discover a real transformation in your love life, in particular, your sex life. A woman's ability to Orgasm, for example, is deeply connected to her state of mind. If you are too busy worrying about your 'flabby bits', you are not 'in the moment' and are preoccupied elsewhere. How on earth do you expect yourself to let go? Let's be brutally honest here, when you are in the throws of passion, do you seriously think that *any* man *is* going to be analysing your body and thinking of anything other than his pleasure? So why on earth would you be denying yourself just as much pleasure, if not more? Again– one word, guilt.

We are pre-programmed to believe that we should 'keep our hands off our tuppenny bits' and that it is 'dirty' to actually enjoy any sexual pleasure. With so much old school guilt swimming around in our heads, it's no wonder that so many of us almost resist letting ourselves go, and truly losing self control.

And it's not just guilt is it. Fear comes into play too – let's be straight here, Men have played their part in the ages, of shaping the way that women feel that they should be, when it comes to the bedroom department. If a woman enjoys sex, she risks being branded as a 'slut', a 'real goer' by the guy who has dumped her. There is this ongoing conflict between the role that a woman should play, and how to strike the balance right. 'A woman should be a cook in the kitchen, and a whore in the bedroom' is a joke often thrown around between the sexes, but then thinking about it logically in between laughs, we wonder 'says who?'. I am pretty damn sure that it was not a woman who came up with that suggestion!

So then, comes the other emotions, resentment may creep in, as we start to listen to the feminist inside of us, who sneers at the thought of us giving a man exactly what we he wants.Some women swing to the other end of the spectrum, and refuse to partake in the art of seduction, or wear sexy underwear, because they see it as 'pleasing the man'. So in this sea of contradictory emotion, it's no wonder that many of us hold back and never truly experience 'pure, unadulterated sexual pleasure'.

The Solution? Simple – like with every other area of your life that we have discussed so far, STOP listening to the external and internal chitter chatter, STOP over analysing everything, and STOP listening to guilt and fear! STOP choosing to play the Victim, the role of the Victim is not welcome in life, but it is most certainly not welcome in the bedroom.

YOU are entitled to be whoever and whatever you want to be when it comes to getting naked with another person, be it man *or* woman. There is no ideal way for things to be done, because we are all individuals, we all have different tastes, and what turns one of us *on,* may be another's turn *off.* Now this isn't rocket science, and some of what I am stating, is obvious to the best of us. So why is it, that we (yes, even me!) still buy magazines, and look at how to be what we think we should be in bed? An article will only ever be written from the writer's point of view, based upon their taste and preferences. Instead of seeking suggestions, why not be the writer of your *own* sex article? What do YOU like? What would YOU recommend for others to try out? No body works the same as another, so this really is down to you to figure out.

Write your own sex article

Just as I suggested above, you are now going to write your own sex article.

Think about making it around 500 words long, and look at areas such as:

- *Seduction and setting the mood*
- *Clothing, underwear, toys and accessories*
- *Pleasure for him*
- *Pleasure for her*

BUT – do not write what you think you should write. Nobody else will see this. Like all of the other exercises in this book, this is about you opening up to yourself, no holds barred. So, the topics are going to look at what YOU enjoy, what YOU like to wear in the bedroom, and so on and if you have held back up until now, then think about what you would like to enjoy or wear, and use this almost like a goal setting task, so that you can begin to **visualise** these changes taking place and create the sex life that you have always desired.

When you have completed this exercise (and if you really are not one for writing, do not worry about the word limit, just go with your flow), store it away, give yourself a couple of days break from it, and then go back and read it with fresh eyes, as though you were reading someone else's article, looking to take their advice. Because let's be honest, we are all so ready to take anyone else's advice at the drop of a hat if it is there in print, so why not listen to your own?

Only when you have a clear idea of what you like, what

*you want to try, what turns you on – will you be able to
start to make it happen'*

Quite frankly, it's about time that some of us ladies, took a little
advice from the Mistress/Dominatrix's out there. Lying back and
hoping that your guy will deliver the goods that you desire, is
like waiting for the sky to turn Golden. Communication is key
when it comes to getting what you want and desire in the
bedroom, and it seems that both sexes are so busy worrying
about pleasing the other, that they lose the moment, and in
some cases, the erection! What's with all of this playing hard
to get out there these days? Seriously – we cannot say what
we want, yet when we do not get what we want, we
complain, and someone ends up frustrated or dumped?

Ladies– tell your guy what turns you on. If you do not have
good communication then maybe you shouldn't be having sex
with whoever anyway.

If you really feel embarrassed about doing this, then you can
communicate with actions, rather than words. If you have a
specific fantasy, then surprise him/her and set up the scenario
and act it out. Now, I am not suggesting that you suddenly
turn into Miss Whiplash, or dabble in the dark and wonderful
world of fetish. That is a personal choice. But why not try out
the following exercise, and see where it takes you?

Sensual Seduction

As the title suggests, you are going to think about seduction
but combining the use of the five senses. I intend to keep this
lighthearted because I want you to feel comfortable at 'having
a go', and not be put off in any way shape or form.

The purpose of this exercise, is not to focus on pleasing another, or go looking for a sexual encounter. Do not worry if you are single, this may only come in handy in the future, it's okay if you don't want to do this, it's not compulsory.

The idea is, that you are able to let go of your inhibitions and feel more confident in the bedroom, and also enable yourself to experience being 'in control'.

Before I go through the exercise with you, I want us just to pause for a moment and consider what it means to 'be in control'. Control is something that in many areas of life, I do my best to try and avoid it. Without thinking too deeply, quickly jot down what comes to mind when YOU hear the word 'Control'.

Control is

....

For me, control brings up memories of a long term relationship that I was in. It also makes me think of school, work, the government. Control has so many negative connotations attached to it that it is a word that is often feared. Control often comes attached to the notion of there being a lack of choice or freedom. However, if you think about it logically, we all have to implement some form of control into our daily lives, otherwise nothing would ever get done. For example, if we were not in control in the kitchen, then food would constantly burn. If we were not in control of our hygiene then others would not want to come near us. Okay, so these examples may raise a giggle, but whether we like it or not, even the most liberated of the bunch have to exert some level of control in their personal day to day choices.

Through the recognition of our now favourite motto, '**you cannot alter the direction of the wind, but you can always adjust your sails**' it makes clearer sense that trying to gain control over life, and those around you, is never a favourable move. But if things are not going your way, particularly in your love area, then how about looking at how you work in relation to the other person? Before throwing down the gauntlet and screaming in desperation, have a look at the role that YOU play in the satisfaction gained from a personal relationship.

As I mentioned in Section Three, in relation to how we interact with others – it is all too easy to look to other people to make us happy, and then complain and feel empty when they don't. WE have more responsibility and power than anyone else has, over our personal happiness. We have the power of communication, and if we are not happy, and want something to change, then our partner will not be aware of this unless we tell them. Sure, it can take a lot of courage to just lay your cards on the table, but again, this is a case of allowing fear to breed, and no true Vixen grants that! Pushing through the fear, and your personal comfort zone is a wonderful opportunity for growth, and the buzz that you get when you do it, is something that can become addictive!

If you are not happy with things in your love life, in particular the bedroom, then YOU have the power to spice things up a little. Taking control in a sexy way, is possibly the only form of control that is acceptable to be inflicted upon another, It may feel a little bit daunting, but think of it as lavishing yourself upon your lucky partner! He or she will get to see you at your most confident best, and will be able to enjoy an hour of sheer pleasure. I am not talking whips, BDSM or pain here – but a little tie and tease, so that you are able to explore and demonstrate, what it is that you truly desire.

On that note, let's look at how you can become the Mistress of your very own pleasure! (and your partners of course, oops!)

What you may need *(I say may as this is down to personal preference and these tools are simply suggestions)*
- *Something that makes you feel Goddess like – your most fabulous seduction outfit*
- *A pair of handcuffs or scarf to be used for tying your partners hands together*
- *A blindfold – one of those eye masks that we use at bed time or on flights is a great alternative and easier to get on and off*
- *Massage Oil (you can even make your own using a base oil and a few drops of rose, lavender and patchouli)*
- *Strawberries, melted chocolate and two glasses of your preferred tipple*

Preparation: Before you begin to think about performing like a seductress, let's work on helping you *feel* like one. Forget analysing how you look on the outside. Your partner is with you because they like, love and accept you for being you. It is not them that you need to convince! Remember that sexiness is an attitude and **attitudes are contagious. Is yours worth catching?** Relaxing and letting yourself enjoy the moment actually inspires and arouses your partner. Let's be realistic here, your partner most likely spends a great deal of time worrying about whether or not he or she satisfies you. If you are distracted by how you feel about yourself, this energy, the vibe of your attitude, will be felt by your partner and this can affect their energy levels. So relaxing and making the most of the moment, is not something that you should feel guilty about – having pleasure from sharing your mind, body and soul, with another human being is a privilege that should be treasured.

Take time to unwind, maybe run yourself a nice bath and add some relaxing essential oils, such as Lavender, Rose, Patchouli or Ylang Ylang. Ylang Ylang is also an 'aphrodisiac' so should help get you in the mood. Next, take a piece of clear quartz and place it on the bottom of the bath.Candle light is also relaxing, and great at creating an atmosphere, the aim with this preparation is to get yourself in the 'zone' – think back to when you created your Goddess Vision Board and did your Goddess Photo Shoot. Whilst you are relaxing, close your eyes, and imagine that every little drop of built up tension, every little knot of stress, any ounce of negativity, is being drawn to the clear quartz, like moths to a flame. Feel it simply drain from you, and then open your eyes and focus on the flame of the candle. Fire is similar to the sun, in the sense that it is a natural and powerful energiser. Imagine that as you stare into the centre of the flame, the energy gathers together in a ball and like an arrow to an archery board, it directs itself in a perfectly straight line and flows continuously. Once you feel revitalised, dry yourself off, and apply your Goddess Potion, safe in the knowledge that it is coating you with sex appeal and confidence. Massage it in gently and lovingly and appreciate every curve, every inch of your unique, fabulous body!

Dress yourself in whatever makes you feel sensationally sexy, and apply however much make-up you feel most suits you. By now, you will be confident in what brings out your Inner Goddess, and so I won't offer any more guidance, listen to your Goddess and allow her to guide your creativity. Once you have expressed your Inner self externally, join your partner, and how about offering them a massage using some base oil mixed with an essential oil of your preference? Now, don't just sit there frantically rubbing away, take a moment to just breathe and 'feel' your partners presence and energy. Position yourself, sitting behind them, gently place both of your hands on their shoulders, and allow your palms to transfer the energy from within you, to the energy within them.

You may take as long as feels right over this, and adapt this exercise in whatever way that works best for you. The idea is, to generate as much Goddess energy within you, as possible. Think of how your heart chakra has the ability to project that wonderful rainbow of pure love and joy to any other human being. Feel this transference taking place, and if you feel that your energy is low, then visualise the sun or moon, connecting to the cycle, healing you deep within. Once you begin to create energy, imagine that your internal 'powerhouse' is generating constantly. Feel the current pass around your body, and pass this on to your partner before you. You are sharing energy and this experience can be extremely magical and bonding, if you allow yourself to completely lose control and just 'go with the flow' of the energy.

Tune into your partner's breathing – not only can you read their current state of well being, you can also adjust your rhythm so that are mirroring them. They may not pick up on it consciously, but subconsciously, this tells your partner that you are completely in tune with them, and it creates a shared union and promotes a feeling of peace. Channel your energy from your Inner Goddess, up into your heart chakra, and allow it to flow along through your arms, oozing from your hands and imagine it infusing them with nothing but sheer love and passion.

Reiki is a spiritual practise that was developed in 1922, by Japanese Buddhist, *Mikao Usui*. It implements a technique that is often referred to as 'palm healing', whereby a practitioner transfers an energy known as *Ki* to the receiver via the palm of his or her hands. In today's modern day world, it is offered as an alternative medicine, that can be used for unblocking the chakras, and balancing one's energy, thus aiding in physical and emotional repair and well being. The technique that I have described for you to perform above, is in essence, a practical form of Reiki. Not only will your partner feel relaxed, they will also benefit from the healing power that you as an individual have to offer – we ALL have this ability.

Allow your massage to flow from this position, to having your partner lay face down, and then simply follow your Goddesses instructions. She will know where to take you, and you will mostly be working in harmony with your partners rhythm. If you begin to feel sexual, and aroused, even better, and I am not about to start describing what you should or should not do, should the mood arise and take you! I am simply offering suggestions but the ultimate goal of this exercise, is for you to feel like a Goddess, and to seduce your partner rather than the other way round. How quickly this happens, is not something to be scripted.

Next, you may want to tie their hands together *lightly* which of course, may come as a little surprise for them if they are not used to such action, but try not to lose the moment, just whisper to them that they're fine, and you are going to give them a treat of their life time. Cover their eyes with the blindfold, and then roll them over so that they are lay on their back. Your partner can now only rely on the senses of taste, touch (but through feeling), sound and smell.

You can now use your imagination, allow your Goddess to guide you, and seduce your partner by running your fingers up and down their body, peeling off their clothes,feeding them the berries, dribbling cool wine along their body and licking it off, and of course, do not forget the art of kissing.

Kissing is a mode through which the Goddess can express herself, so don't just use it as a 'way in', see it as an art form in itself. Take the lead, and set a pace and rhythm, and get your partner to follow. If they are racing ahead with no real patience, then tease them by pulling away for a second, and keep doing this to show them that you are in the lead. Take it slow, and increase the rhythm in time to your joint arousal. Kissing is almost like a secret hidden language that can only be understood by your lover. Communicate through your kissing, exactly what is on your mind.

If you feel *comfortable,* you may like to whisper to your partner, what it is that you like about their body, or tease them by asking them to guess what you may do to them next. This can be a great way to find out what their fantasy is, and also the perfect arena within which you can take the lead and tell them, *whilst maybe demonstrating* exactly what it is that YOU desire. This enables communication to take place, without there being any awkward silences, or without it feeling pre-meditated and as though you had been planning to bring the matter up. We all know how this can sometimes lead to one person feeling like they are being set upon, so this takes away the risk of any arguments.

The whole experience is great for you, because your partner has their eyes covered, and so you can take this as far as you wish to go, maybe even take the lead and *you* make love to your partner. How many times have you shied away from going on top because you are too aware of your flabby bits, small breasts – whatever your hang up is ? Or are you someone who is embarrassed to perform oral sex on your partner, because you are too aware of them watching you? An awful lot of our hang-ups do come about from wondering how we look, and this lack of confidence is attached to Fear.

This exercise is not eradicating fear in an instant, because when it comes to love making, nothing is that simple or immediate . But, it gives you the opportunity to lose control, to truly let your hair down, and take the lead.It will boost your confidence no end, and you can adapt this time and time again, until you feel comfortable to take those cuffs and that blindfold off part way through, by which time you won't be nervous, because you will be so turned on that your mind will be elsewhere.

Role play is also another area that opens the doors for communication and confidence building. You can almost lose yourself in another character and explore the different traits that your character would have, without looking like you have gone completely bonkers. For example, dressing as a

Dominatrix, puts you in the drivers seat but dressing as a secretary allows you to explore your submissive side.

Unleashing your Inner Goddess is not all about you taking the lead – it is about finding the areas that feel most natural or intriguing to you and then exploring them as and when you feel ready.

I am not suggesting that the Goddess in you has to be some sort of Mistress of the night. This is not exclusively set to you playing the role of the leader. But through trying out such a character, even if just for one night, it gives rise to you communicating about what you both want and like, and allows you to take away your confidence issues and your body worries for a temporary moment, in order to begin to re-frame things and work on them via whatever avenues come about from this experience.

Only when you are truly comfortable with yourself in the bedroom can you enter the wonderful world of your most intense orgasms.

But I am not taking you down the road in this book. Oh no – that is reserved for another book in its own right, Orgasms and sexual techniques and positions are more suited to a 'how to' sex manual. The advice that I will give you now, is that there are no rights and wrongs in the bedroom. What takes place between you and your partner/s is a private arena within which you both work out what does and does not turn you on, *together.* The most important point that I want you to take away from any section of this book, is that your life will turn around for the better, in all areas, as soon as you stop looking for the answers externally and start listening to the advice of the one internally – Your Inner Goddess! When we busy our minds with the idea that we should be this, that or the other, we lose sight of who we are already. And when and only when, we are our most authentic self, will we attract the life and the people who are most suited to *us*. Until we master this, we will be caught in an ongoing cycle of situations and people that somehow don't sit right. We will go round and round in circles, looking for the reason, trying to find the answer, when the key to personal freedom and transformation is and has always been , *within ourselves.*

Before we say goodbye – I want to thank you for giving me the chance to hopefully inspire you to embark upon your personal journey with your head held high! The information that I offer to you, is simply the way that I see the world through *my* eyes. Never forget, that we can only ever do things *our* way. Make like a sponge, and absorb all of the information that this world has to offer you. If something feels right, then follow it, if something feels wrong, question why, or take an alternative route. Your Inner Goddess is the one thing that remains constant in these times of change and as long as you stay connected to her, then you will be guided down the path that is intended for you. There are no rights and wrongs, the key to a happy and 'effortless' life is to simply rely upon YOU. The journey may be colourful and it may not be plain sailing, but 'you cannot alter the direction of the wind, but you can always adjust your sails'. You will be just fine, even when the chips are down, because the human spirit, the feminine energy is designed to simply survive. Aside from the release through death, when our time on earth is over, there is very little choice in the fact that life will throw us around a bit. So face it head on, with your spirits high, and make of it what you can!

Buddha said on his death bed **'You must be your own lamp and refuge. Take refuge in nothing outside yourself. Hold firm to the Truth as a lamp and a refuge, and do not look for anything as refuge besides yourself'** – trust in your Inner Goddess, allow her to be *your* lamp and refuge. May her magnificent energy illuminate the truth, and keep out the darkness. Allow her light to radiate from within to without, let her guide your way, and in times of struggle, seek refuge in her bosom, knowing that she will protect you in all weathers. There is no other truth but that of your own. A life spent following the guidance of others, is a life spent pursuing anothers dreams. Now is the time to embrace the journey on the Ocean of Life – may you as your vessel carry your spirit to inner peace and wisdom. Shedding your old skin, peeling away the layers and finally being your most authentic self, you are free to release the past, focus in the present, and create the tomorrow that your heart desires. Stop existing, it's time to start LIVING!

THE GODDESS GUIDE TO LOTIONS, POTIONS AND ALL THINGS MAGICKAL

Though out the book I suggest throwing in a little help from all things weird and wonderful, in order to help access your Inner Goddess. Here is a quick reminder of some things that you may find useful, both in the present and in the future. I have complied this here, so that you can refer to it with ease.

Goddess Candles
Red: Love, passion, self confidence, desire, seduction
Pink: self love, self confidence, self healing, romance, friendship, compassion, connection
White: Cleansing, Purifying, Clarity, Protection, Wisdom, Focus
Black: Protection, removing negativity, protection from evil
Purple: the colour of female intuition, wisdom, feminine power, the divine Goddess

Goddess Crystals
Rose Quartz: Love and calm. Rose quartz is one of the most popular crystals along with amethyst and clear quartz. It has a calming and soothing energy. It promotes self-love and helps overcome feelings of not being 'good' enough, self-criticism and resentment. It reminds us that when you love yourself and are happy in the moment there is no need for haste. Rose quartz embraces the one true currency of life, love.

Clear Quartz: One of the most powerful all rounders, great for general healing and purifying, helps you to connect your Inner self. Clear quartz helps to dispel negative energy you may have absorbed from other people. If you tend to put yourself down, quartz may help you fight that feeling. It is good to hold or have around whenever you feel foggy, uncertain or would like to see your way more clearly. It is one of the most frequently used crystals because of its wide-ranging benefits.

Citrine: the sunshine stone, also known as the 'cuddle stone' is like a big comforting hug! Citrine is a stone that often reflects light in a sunny and warming fashion. It is a crystal of creativity and positive expression of who we truly are. This gives us a good feeling and impacts on those around us in a positive way.

Amethyst: & nbsp; reminds us of the spiritual thread that runs through our life and can be used as a tool to aid spiritual awakening and intuition. Amethyst can bring a calming influence and therefore be of great help in times of change. It's excellent to hold or have by you when you're practising meditation and when placed in a room it can help absorb negativity. Placed under the pillow it may help you sleep better.

Goddess Motto's
'You cannot alter the direction of the wind, but you can always adjust your sails'

'Be the change that you wish to see in the world' – Ghandi

'Be your own lamp, be your own refuge' – Buddha

'In your darkest hour, you'll find gold'

Goddess Lotion:
Olive Oil, sea salt (a few handfuls) and some lavender oil. Mix it all together, keep in a glass bottle and store in a cool place

Goddess Potion:
A bland, base cream that you can get from a chemist or aromatherapist. To it, add some oils that inspire you: I like rose, lavender, geranium. A dash of ylang ylang is great for sex appeal. Again, store in a glass bottle as this contains essential oils that can permeate plastic.

Goddess Secret Weapons:
Stockings, heels, garter, lipstick, Goddess Potion, The sun and moon as emergency energy sources – add to this list as you discover things that work for YOU

NOTES

We hope that you have enjoyed this book. To keep up to date with Angela's adventures and to get free advice and tips, head to www.everywomanssecretweapon.co.uk and www.everywomanssecretweapon.com

You can keep track of forthcoming talks, and the expected release date of Angela's second book titled 'Avoiding Mr Right – The real path to finding love?' Which is due for release in 2011 by Crabtree Press.

Crabtree Press